THE GLORIOUS RETURN
of
KING JESUS

The Rapture and The Great Tribulation

An honest search for biblical truth.

Ben R. Peters

The Glorious Return of King Jesus
@2023 by Ben R. Peters

Author grants permission for any non-commercial reproduction to promote the Kingdom of God. All rights reserved.

Published by
Kingdom Sending Center
P.O. Box 25
Genoa, IL 60135

www.kingdomsendingcenter.org
ben.peters@kingdomsendingcenter.org

Print edition ISBN: 9798398150988

All scripture quotations, unless otherwise indicated, are taken from the New King James Version ©1982 by Thomas Nelson, Inc. Used by permission. All rights reserved.

Cover design by Jessica Seiler.

ACKNOWLEDGEMENTS

1. First and foremost, I want to acknowledge the Holy Spirit for helping me to ask the right questions and leading me to the answers.

2. My parents: who taught me to read and memorize Scripture as a child some 70 years ago.

3. My wife, Brenda: who encourages me, often prophetically, and allows me to hide away and interact with others to get this book finished.

4. My Kingdom Sending Center team: including our indispensable, pure-hearted, gifted, and loyal ministry assistant, Lyn Jackson. Also, my awesome proofreading, editing, and formatting expert, Carole Robbins, with significant assistance from her talented husband, Bruce. Finally, I was blessed with the services of our website expert, Jennifer Song, who had to leave the project when emergency family situations called her away.

I say a huge thanks to each one of you, and to others I haven't named, who helped us get this project going. May you all be greatly rewarded!

CONTENTS

PREFACE:	KEEPING HEARTS AND MINDS OPEN AND LOVING	1
CHAPTER 1	CAN'T FIND "LEFT BEHIND"	10
CHAPTER 2	COMING AGAIN, AGAIN? THE LAST TRUMPET DILEMMA	21
CHAPTER 3	IT'S ABOUT HIS COMING – NOT OUR GOING	28
CHAPTER 4	UNANSWERED QUESTIONS IN DANIEL AND REVELATION	38
CHAPTER 5	THE RESTRAINING - WHO IS TAKEN OUT OF THE WAY?	46
CHAPTER 6	NOT APPOINTED TO WRATH AND THE OPEN DOOR	53
CHAPTER 7	A POWERFUL PROPHETIC TYPE AND SHADOW	64
CHAPTER 8	WHERE ARE WE NOW? COMFORTING CONCLUSIONS	90

PREFACE:

KEEPING HEARTS AND MINDS OPEN AND LOVING

Writing a book about the "rapture" is not something I do without serious misgivings or concerns. In public meetings, I have mostly avoided sharing my beliefs. Brenda and I have too many friends whom we deeply love, who have always been taught a different scenario than what I now teach, and I never want to offend them. They have been drawn to our ministry because it has been one of encouragement and healing, especially with the personal prophetic words we have shared. I don't want my views on eschatology to destroy our friendships or bring about a spirit of contention between us.

So, in light of the above, why would I tackle this subject in a book and risk alienating so many Christians? I guess the answer is simply that God's people make choices and decisions in life regularly, based upon what they believe regarding God's plans for their future. If they are being taught something that is in error, they may logically make wrong choices and decisions, which could rob both them and Christ's Kingdom of many blessings. Thus, as a servant

The Glorious Return of King Jesus

of Jesus, I shouldn't simply try to avoid conflict and not offend people. My purpose should be to teach the truth from God's Word, so that people can truly make the right choices and decisions. We will expand on this throughout the book.

As a life-long student, and ultimately a teacher of God's Word, I've learned to ask questions, when it seems like questions should be asked. Having been raised in churches that taught about a Pre-Tribulation Rapture, I have asked a lot of questions regarding the various aspects of that teaching. It led me to do a lot of searching for confirmation. What I quickly discovered was that there were many, many questions without good answers in the teachings of others that I had heard throughout my childhood and youth. This book deals with many of those questions, and I humbly appeal to every reader to do their own research to confirm or refute my findings.

I also want to ask every reader to pray for a hungry heart and an open mind for the truth of God's Word. I apologize, in advance, for any harshness or attitudes of intellectual or religious superiority that may come across from the way my points are expressed. I will do my best to avoid letting this happen.

Understanding eschatology, the study of the end times, is not the most important doctrine or teaching of the church. Relationship with our Creator, Lord and Savior, the Father, Son, and Holy Spirit is what Christianity is all about. And GOD IS LOVE!!! This relationship is all about LOVE, and

Preface

that is what this writer desires with his readers. Can we still fervently love each other, even if we disagree on this particular teaching? I trust so. Even more, I trust that the information shared in this small book will be convincing enough that the reader will, for the sake of Christ's Kingdom expansion, come into agreement with what the Bible actually teaches about this subject.

I also strongly desire to impart more hope than anxiety and fear. I want every believer to understand that Jesus has promised never to leave us or forsake us. Even in the Valley of the Shadow of Death, our Shepherd is right there with us. His angels will assist us in every situation, and we will always have the Holy Spirit to teach, guide, and comfort us. His gifts and fruit will never be withdrawn, so we can always be confident that even if persecution arises, God's grace will always be sufficient, and we will be more than conquerors through Him who loves us.

In addition to that, we know that both our evil enemy and his agent, the antichrist have a very limited time to do their worst to destroy and defeat us. We will have all of eternity to rejoice in God's grace and His goodness to us. There is nothing that can separate us from His love, according to Paul in Romans 8:35-39.

DISCLAIMER:

#1. This book is quite limited in its scope regarding end-time events. This author does not claim to be an end-time scholar. Our focus is simply on one event, and whether it has truly been biblically based or not. Frankly put, I DO NOT have strong opinions regarding many other end-time events, and I am still very open to learning from others in the Kingdom. Prophetic passages in Scripture can be extremely complicated to interpret. God made it intentionally difficult for obvious reasons.

Like the Pharisees, many scholars think they can figure out everything in Scripture through academic excellence. But prophetic passages can have multiple applications, some local and others universal, some immediate, some in the near future, and some potentially hundreds or thousands of years in the future, as we shall see.

Of one thing, I am sure. No Bible scholar has all the truth, no matter how great a scholar he or she is. God won't give it all to one person, and the truth can't all be discovered through scholarship as we stated above. I believe that God reveals His secrets to those who love Him, when He is ready to do so. Even Jesus didn't know when He would return, and the prophets could only guess as to the timing of most of their prophetic words. I believe in the "Unity of the Body" concept, where God will reveal one nugget of truth to one and another nugget to someone else. He wants us to need each other and to bring all our gifts and knowledge together, so that we truly function as the "Body of Christ," where each member has a function that is important and needed. This takes a deeper level of humility than what commonly manifests in Christ's body, today.

Preface

#2. I am well aware of the fact that many people have come to a saving knowledge of Jesus, as Lord and Savior, through the various books and movies released with the teaching that I am about to challenge in the pages of this book. Many have accepted Christ because of the fear of having to go through the Great Tribulation. It is true that the "Fear of the Lord is the beginning of wisdom." I thank God for the fact that He can use partial truths to draw souls to Himself. At the same time, the truth that Jesus is coming back to judge the world should also instill the "Fear of the Lord" in all believers. But even more importantly, the knowledge that God wants to be a personal Friend, who never leaves or forsakes us, should give us the strength and courage to face anything on this earth, until He comes to overpower His enemy and ours.

#3. I am not attempting, in this book, to do a thorough Genesis - Revelation analysis of every related Bible passage. I want to make this easy for the reader to read and follow the logic. My personal qualifications to write on this particular subject would be my seven decades of reading and studying God's Word, along with over fifty-five years as a preacher and teacher of the gospel. For those looking for academic credentials, I have two degrees, including a Master of Divinity degree (MDiv), from Canadian Theological Seminary, in Regina, Saskatchewan, Canada. But probably the biggest qualification, to go along with the biblical training, is the "gift of curiosity" that God gave me, which motivates me to ask questions and seek answers.

The Glorious Return of King Jesus

TO THOSE WHO ARE CURIOUS, BUT NOT BIBLE SCHOLARS OR EVEN BIBLE BELIEVERS:

We sincerely desire that you read this book with an open mind and ultimately find some answers to your questions regarding what the future holds for you in this troubled world. To start with, allow me to define some of the terms we will be using throughout this short book.

SOME IMPORTANT DEFINITIONS:

#1. THE PRE-TRIBULATION RAPTURE

The word "RAPTURE" is not a Bible word, but it is a word used by many Christians to describe what they believe will happen when Jesus returns to earth. They believe the Bible says that Jesus will gather up His followers, taking them to Heaven for either three and a half or seven years, while the rest of the world experiences what is referred to as "The Great Tribulation."

The rapture doctrine is actually less than 200 years old. However, a majority of evangelical Christians have embraced it, because it certainly appears to be a better option than living through any portion of the Great Tribulation.

There is also a "Mid-Tribulation Rapture Theory," which postulates that Jesus will remove His saints in the middle of the seven-year period, before things get really bad.

Preface

#2. THE SECOND COMING

The phrase "Second Coming" is a general term that refers to Jesus' return to earth to establish a one-thousand-year Kingdom reign. His "First Coming" was two thousand years ago, when He was born in Bethlehem. Those who believe in The Rapture Theory see The Second Coming as a two-part event. This doctrine incorporates the first return as the Rapture, before or during "The Great Tribulation," with the second return occurring after "The Great Tribulation."

Those who do not believe The Rapture Theory, including this author, believe Jesus returns only once. Then the living saints rise to meet Him in the air, to usher Him into Jerusalem, while those who have died and spent time in Heaven return to earth with resurrected bodies, so they can live on the earth.

#3. THE MILLENNIUM

In Christian circles, The Millennium refers to a period of one thousand years, during which Jesus is King over all the earth, and those who serve Jesus will rule and reign with Him. The devil has been bound and thrown into a bottomless pit at this time, awaiting his release (Revelation 20:1-3). When Jesus initially returns to earth, He destroys the antichrist and judges the wicked. The thousand years that follow will be marked by peace and prosperity on earth.

#4. LEFT BEHIND

This is a phrase made popular in recent books and movies, which was adapted from Jesus' teachings in Matthew 24. Rapture theorists believe that some will be taken to Heaven when Jesus comes, while others will be left behind to endure the Great Tribulation. This is actually the reverse of the true interpretation of what Jesus was teaching.

#5. THE GREAT TRIBULATION

This phrase, taken primarily from Matthew 24:21, is seen by most scholars as a period of either three and a half or seven years, in which the "man of sin" or "the antichrist" has total control of the world. He institutes global laws, requiring a "mark" on the hand or forehead, to enable a person to buy or sell anything. It will be the world-wide control of all peoples and resources. The antichrist will proclaim himself the savior of the human race, and he will persecute all Christian believers.

#6. THE END TIMES

This is a general catch-all phrase, which refers to a period of time when the current era has passed, and a new era has come. It deals with events talked about in Scripture that will take place, including just before, during and after Christ's return. The Bible speaks about the rise of world leaders, wars, and cataclysmic events, leading up to the return of Jesus. It includes the years of tribulation and the

Preface

establishment of Christ's Kingdom on the earth. Of course, it means different things to the various streams of Christendom.

#7. PRETERITE AND PARTIAL-PRETERITE POSITIONS

The word "Preterite" is a grammatical term, referring to past, or completed past events. When these terms are used in eschatological discussions, they refer to events that have already been partially or completely fulfilled. More specifically, it refers to the Great Tribulation having already happened, or at least having been partially fulfilled. This position is embraced by those who believe the worst is over and things will get better until Jesus returns.

As we proceed, we are about to challenge the views and beliefs of many Christians, but we encourage every reader to keep an open mind and weigh the evidence honestly and prayerfully. Personally, I have tried to do the same.

With these points in mind, we will jump right into this subject by exposing one of the most obvious and glaringly false interpretations of a Bible passage that I have ever seen.

CHAPTER ONE

CAN'T FIND "LEFT BEHIND"

Are you tired of the stresses of life? Have you been deeply saddened or brokenhearted over the loss of friends and loved ones? Have you experienced physical and emotional pain from things that blindsided you in life? I believe we all have, and it's clear that life on this planet is not easy or without pain for virtually everyone.

But we who know Jesus as Savior and Lord have something awesome to get excited about. Jesus is coming as our triumphant King to conquer the enemy. He's coming to stop your pain, take your stress, comfort your heart, and wipe every tear from your eyes. He's coming back to take control and end the reign of evil in this world. He will judge the wicked and remove them, so they can no longer affect us, and it may be sooner than we think. There will truly be "Peace on Earth, Good Will Toward Men."

However, we must be prepared for some bumps in the road before that wonderful day arrives. There are a few events on God's calendar that we need to be prepared for. While some believe that Christians won't experience trials and testing, we'd rather you were forewarned and prepared than shocked and disillusioned.

DO YOU WANT TO BE "LEFT BEHIND?"

Most church-going Christians would definitely say, "No, I don't want to be left behind." They've seen all the movies or read the books portraying that being left behind is a terrible thing to be avoided at all costs.

If I were to ask 100 church-going evangelical or charismatic Christians where in the Bible they found the phrase "LEFT BEHIND," perhaps five would say in Matthew 24. Most couldn't tell me where to find it, but they would swear it was in the Bible somewhere. At the most, perhaps one or two would say it wasn't in the Bible.

Actually, I did find two places in Scripture where the phrase "Left Behind" is used. They are both in the Old Testament, so they are not where one would expect them to be found. In Exodus 10:26, Moses said, *"Our cattle also shall go with us; there shall not a hoof be LEFT BEHIND."* Obviously, not exactly a great verse to base a rapture theory on.

This phrase was mentioned for the second time in I Samuel 30:9, *"So David went, he and the six hundred men who were with him, and came to the brook Besor, where those stayed who were LEFT BEHIND."* This verse also seems to have nothing to do with the concept of the Rapture, because the two hundred men who were "left behind," were the ones that were too weak and exhausted to chase after the enemy. They had to rest while four hundred men pursued the enemy who had stolen all their possessions and taken their wives, sons, and daughters into captivity.

So, seriously, where did the phrase "Left Behind" come from, as it relates to The Rapture? And how did the book writers and filmmakers get it so very wrong? Let's take a look at what Matthew 24 actually says, focusing in on the "Days of Noah" reference, which is the supposed source of the phrase "Left Behind." We'll come back to Matthew 24 later, to deal with other rapture issues.

Matthew 24:

24:37	*"But as the days of Noah were, so also will the coming of the Son of Man be.*
24:38	*For as in the days before the flood, they were eating and drinking, marrying and giving in marriage, until the day that Noah entered the ark,*
24:39	*And did not know until the flood came and took them all away, so also will the coming of the Son of Man Be.*
24:40	*Then two men will be in the field: one will be taken and the other left.*
24:41	*Two women will be grinding at the mill: one will be taken and the other left.*
24:42	*Watch therefore, for you do not know what hour your Lord is coming."*

First of all, please note that the word "BEHIND" is not in the passage at all.

Most importantly, notice the words "took" and "taken." The people didn't listen to Noah and were left out of the ark, and Verse 39 says the flood took them away. The disobedient were the ones who were taken.

Thus, the word "taken" clearly means that their lives were taken from them. They were judged by God for their evil ways and drowned in the flood. They certainly were not taken to Heaven to avoid The Tribulation.

With this being extremely clear and undeniable, then the verses that follow must be interpreted like this:

"Two men will be in the field. One will be taken out, or suddenly judged. The other will be left alive, like Noah in the ark."

"Two women will be grinding at the mill. One will be taken out, or suddenly judged, and the other will be left alive."

And yet, the very opposite is being taught in books and movies. How can this be? That's a question that the authors of the "Left Behind" series should answer, but I'm willing to speculate on this. Since around 1830, the idea of an "escape rapture" has grown in popularity. The idea of escaping the "Great Tribulation" was a welcomed concept. Who wouldn't choose Heaven over this time of trouble and sorrow under a cruel and evil antichrist?

The Glorious Return of King Jesus

Because 1 Thessalonians tells us that we will rise to meet Jesus in the air, Bible teachers were looking for passages indicating that some would go up, while others remained on earth to suffer the Great Tribulation. Without paying attention to the context, the passage in Matthew 24 fits that bill. One was taken (supposedly to Heaven) and the other left behind on the earth to suffer in the Great Tribulation.

NOTE: There is quite a bit of information available about the origins of the "escape rapture" theory on the internet. The details are not always confirmed, but there is certainly debate about the details, since the story goes back to around 1828-1830. Apparently, the prophetic word originated from a 15-year-old named Margaret Macdonald, who believed that only a few would be taken up to Heaven, while most Christians would remain. Over time, that aspect was forgotten, and now all believers are expecting to be "raptured."

Other than the passage in 1 Thessalonians 4:15-17, Matthew 24 is probably the most used to promote the "escape rapture" theory. As we will see in following chapters, neither of these passages talk about Christians going to Heaven during the Great Tribulation mentioned in Matthew 24:21.

SUBCONSCIOUS MOTIVATION TO BELIEVE WHAT ONE DESIRES

I'll never forget reading an essay by William James, for a university philosophy class assignment. The essay was entitled "The Will to Believe." The main thesis of the essay was that our desire to believe something will often overrule our ability to reason logically to a conclusion that we do not desire.

EVOLUTION:

Thus, we find people, including highly educated teachers and professors, while professing themselves to be wise, embracing an extremely foolish and illogical theory. Rather than accepting the obvious truth that there is a Creator – an intelligent Being who designed the universe and living beings, they prefer to accept the incomprehensible notion that, "In the beginning, there was nothing. And then suddenly, without any warning, that nothing exploded into something." That "nothing" in the Big Bang explosion, produced an infinitesimally large amount of mass to fill the universe with stars and galaxies.

These massive "somethings" were made up of intricately designed and infinitesimally tiny bits of matter, called atoms, which in turn were made up of even tinier particles, now known as electrons, neutrons, protons, and photons. These atoms formed compounds with other atoms from different elements, such as hydrogen, oxygen, nitrogen, carbon, silicone, sodium, chlorine, silver, gold, etc. They did so by sharing electrons with atoms that had a compatible ring of electrons. The results were compounds such as H_2O (water), $NaCl$ (salt), H_2SO_4 (sulfuric acid), and countless thousands of other complex combinations.

Any "supposedly" intelligent being who believes this mysterious explosion of "nothing" produced an enormous amount of "something" presents powerful proof, as described in the thesis of William James, that our will to believe trumps our ability to reason logically to a sound conclusion. I could go on and on about the incredible creativity required to form our individual DNA, etc., but we must ask the obvious question, which is, "Why are they so foolish?" Before we answer that question, let's move on to another example of the power of the will to believe.

CESSATIONISM:

The doctrine of cessationism is taught and accepted by many top theologians of our day, especially in the more liberal and evangelical, non-Pentecostal or charismatic churches. Again, in my opinion, the Bible does not support this teaching at all. However, proponents have found a few verses, which were taken out of context, to support this doctrine that signs and wonders ceased, either after the Bible was complete, or after all the original apostles, including Paul, died. They also deny the contemporary existence of apostles and prophets. There are many varieties of cessationism, but they all basically say that God doesn't operate in the miraculous realm today. It's not just a small segment of the church that accepts this fallacy, it's a very substantial and significant segment of Christian churches.

To prove the falsity of cessationism is not our mission in this book. I would encourage any curious reader to read our earlier book titled *Signs and Wonders – To Seek or Not to Seek*. Our purpose here is to reveal the motivation of theological leaders who have embraced a very untenable doctrine, which I believe is a huge insult to God and a terrible hindrance to building the Kingdom of Heaven on the earth.

So, let's now ask questions regarding both of these examples. Why do evolutionists accept an unproven and frankly ridiculous theory, and why do theologians embrace a terribly unbiblical and hellish doctrine, insulting God's character and handicapping the church in its effectiveness?

The clue to the first question is found in Romans 1:18-32. Man didn't want to acknowledge the existence of a God who could hold them accountable for their actions. Creation had always shouted loudly to them that there had to be a Creator. But their will to believe that He didn't exist, led them to worship and serve many less powerful gods, which were more under their control. They made images of these gods and called them idols. However, when Charles Darwin seemed to suggest an alternative to a "Creator," there was a virtual stampede to sign onto his theory. Darwin's "Origin of Species" was not "The Origin

The Glorious Return of King Jesus

of Matter or Life." It was a theory of how one species might change into another species. Thus, it was the desire of men and women to believe that they were okay living in their sin, which led to the overwhelming acceptance of the ridiculous theory of evolution.

The answer to the second question is quite similar. After the original passion of the apostles and the disciples of Jesus had worn off, His followers had become more and more religious, rather than relational. As a result, the occurrence of supernatural events declined, and signs of spiritual life had dwindled by the dark ages. Religion had taken over and religious rituals were the staple of church life.

Fast forward to 1500 A.D. and observe the church coming back to life. The Bible was becoming available in the language of the people, rather than only in Latin. Doctrines such as "Justification by Faith" were being taught by some. There was an explosion of restored theological truths, but there was little restoration of the lifestyle of the early church with its accompanying miraculous events.

As the Reformation progressed, each movement claimed to have "THE TRUTH." There was a lot of religious pride in their specific restored doctrines. When the subject of the miraculous signs and wonders of the early church came up, most leaders were not humble enough to say, "Where are we failing? Why don't we see the same miracles today?"

The fact is, they wanted to believe they were very spiritual or biblical. This was especially obvious during the Pentecostal movement of the early 1900's. People who were manifesting spiritual gifts in various settings would sometimes come across as spiritually superior to those who didn't. This, of course, strongly agitated the leaders of the various existing denominations. These leaders would strongly react to such insulting attitudes. After all, they had the education and the authority of their church or movement.

Something inside of them was saying that they had to prove they were right and the others wrong. To admit that they were less spiritual than those crazy Pentecostals was too difficult for them, like it was for the Pharisees of Jesus' day. Motivated by the desire to maintain the status quo and not feel inferior, they sought Scriptures to prove that they did not need to change the way they did church. Like the evolutionists who didn't want to admit there was a Being far superior to them, who would hold them accountable, the cessationist theologians wanted an excuse not to believe that the miraculous was for their day.

ESCAPE RAPTURE:

So how does this relate to our subject – The Rapture? It certainly is appealing to our human soul to have a way to escape pain and suffering. If we are given a choice to accept a teaching that removes that potential, most people would take it over a teaching that says tougher times are coming and you're going to have to toughen up.

As I was growing up in a faith-filled Pentecostal home, my parents and other family members, along with all the church people we knew, held onto The Escape Rapture belief. I didn't know anyone who didn't believe in it then. This doctrine had taken the church by storm, and I can only guess the potential negative impact it has had on the church at large. It was only after finishing seminary, where I didn't have any courses on eschatology, that I began to search the Scriptures on my own to examine what the Bible was actually saying.

Like the phrase "Left Behind," I couldn't find any real solid evidence in the prophetic passages indicating an "escape rapture." I'm familiar with the charts and the verses used to support their doctrine. However, with a little scrutiny of the context, there's no actual evidence that Jesus is coming to rescue us from the Great Tribulation.

In the following chapters, we will lay out more of the important questions that need to be asked regarding the current teaching on this subject. Let's begin next by asking whether the "last trump" is actually the last trump, because I see a real problem here. It's another question with no answer.

CHAPTER TWO

COMING AGAIN, AGAIN?
THE LAST TRUMPET DILEMMA

Most Christians have a limited understanding of what events must occur for there to be an "escape rapture" preceding the Great Tribulation. Although there are many different theories and opinions about how things could happen, including the timing and the duration of the tribulation, we will try to give the reader a basic understanding of the various elements of the events that are expected to occur.

The key passages we will look at include 1 Thessalonians 4, 1 Corinthians 15, and Matthew 24. Again, we want to remind the reader that we are not trying to understand everything about the end times. In this chapter, we are asking the question, "Can there be another trumpet after the 'Last Trumpet?'"

Let's begin with the number one rapture passage, **1 Thessalonians 4:13-18:**

4:13   *"But I do not want you to be ignorant, brethren, concerning those who have fallen asleep, lest you sorrow as others who have no hope.*

4:14   *For if we believe that Jesus died and rose again, even so God will bring with Him those who sleep in Jesus.*

4:15   *For this we say to you by the word of the Lord, that we who are alive and remain until the coming of the Lord will by no means precede those who are asleep.*

4:16   *For the Lord Himself will descend from Heaven with a shout, with the voice of an archangel, and with the TRUMPET of God. And the dead in Christ shall rise first.*

4:17   *Then we who are alive and remain shall be caught up together with them in the clouds to meet the Lord in the air. And thus, we shall always be with the Lord.*

4:18   *Therefore comfort one another with these words."*

Please note the reference to the "TRUMPET of God" in verse 16.

Let's now look at **1 Corinthians 15:51-52**:

15:51   *"Behold, I tell you a mystery: We shall not all sleep, but we shall all be changed.*

15:52   *In a moment, in the twinkling of an eye, at the LAST TRUMPET. For the TRUMPET will sound,*

> *and the dead will be raised incorruptible, and we shall be changed."*

I don't believe one can deny that both of these passages (1 Thessalonians and 1 Corinthians) describe the same event. Both passages include the dead being raised and the living receiving resurrected bodies. "WE SHALL ALL BE CHANGED."

Since both the 1 Thessalonians and the 1 Corinthians passages mention the sound of a trumpet, and the latter adds the adjective "LAST," then the trumpet in 1 Thessalonians is obviously referring to the same event and is also the "LAST" trumpet. Therefore, if it's the LAST trumpet in 1 Corinthians, it's also the LAST trumpet in 1 Thessalonians.

The problem with The Escape Rapture Theory is that it teaches that the rapture is the first event, accompanied by the sound of the LAST trumpet. However, Jesus does not come back the second time to set up His Kingdom on earth until the tribulation is past. Now let's go back to Matthew 24 to explore why this issue of the "LAST Trump" is such a problem for The Rapture Theory.

To recap what we've previously shared: the Rapture Theory states that Jesus will come once to snatch us away, and then He returns either three and a half or seven years later to set up His Kingdom.

The Glorious Return of King Jesus

Matthew 24:21-22, 29-31 describes Jesus returning in power and glory to set up His Kingdom:

24:21   *"For then there will be GREAT TRIBULATION, such as has not been since the beginning of the world until this time, no, nor ever shall be.*

24:22   *And unless those days were shortened, no flesh would be saved; but for the elect's sake, those days will be shortened.*

24:29   *Immediately after the tribulation of those days the sun will be darkened, and the moon will not give its light; the stars will fall from heaven, and the powers of the heavens will be shaken.*

24:30   *Then the sign of the Son of Man will appear in heaven, and then all the tribes of the earth will mourn, and they will see the Son of Man coming on the clouds of heaven with power and great glory.*

24:31   *And He will send His angels with a great sound of a TRUMPET, and they will gather together His elect from the four winds, from one end of heaven to the other."*

There are seven conclusions we can draw from the five verses above:

1. Those who died (fallen asleep) are with Jesus in Heaven.
2. When Jesus returns, they will come back with Him.
3. They will be given resurrected bodies.

4. Those believers who are alive at the time will rise to meet Him in the air.
5. They will all join together in the clouds as He returns.
6. We will forever be with the Lord.
7. We can comfort one another knowing He will return.

These verses from Matthew 24 are clearly about Jesus coming back to the earth to rule and to reign. The unrighteous will mourn because they face judgment for their evil deeds. Therefore, according to The Escape Rapture Theory, this is clearly the second "second coming" of Jesus, when He actually touches down on the earth. With that established, please note the reference in verse 31 to the "great sound of a trumpet."

Herein lies the problem for The Rapture Theory. If the first two passages, which we just reviewed, describe an event different from the Matthew 24 event, in which the "last trumpet" sounded, how can there be another later event where a "great sound of a trumpet" is heard?

Not only do we have the problem of the "last trumpet" not being the "last trumpet" after all, but we have words that seem to describe the same event we discussed in the first two passages we looked at. Notice the last part of Matthew 24:31. It talks about Jesus gathering His people to Himself, not just from the earth but "from one end of heaven to the other."

Clearly, the only way for me to understand these passages is to accept the fact that all three are talking about the exact same event. Each one focuses on or includes different aspects of His coming, but they could not be talking about two different events. For me, it's very clear that Jesus returns to earth once and not twice. All three events include a trumpet, and you can't have another trumpet after the "last trumpet."

WHO NEEDS A BODY?

We have established that for The Escape Rapture Theory to be valid, Jesus would have to come again, twice. However, according to the theory, the first time Jesus returns, He will not touch down on the earth. Rather, we who remain, along with the newly resurrected dead, will rise to meet Him in the air. Then all would fly back with Him to a place of safety for either three and a half or seven years, while the Great Tribulation takes place on earth.

The dilemma of the last trumpet is just one problem with this theory. A little common-sense logic, which seems to be lacking in this discussion, gives us another reason to doubt The Rapture Theory. Let's ask this simple question:

If the dead in Christ return with Him to meet us in the air, and do not touch down, but return to where they came from, then why do they need to be resurrected? They have been doing fine in a heavenly body. If they descended in their heavenly body and are returning to where they came from, why do they need a resurrected body? And why do we need a transformed body if we are heading for Heaven, rather than staying on earth?

It seems to me to make much more sense that we would all get new bodies, like Jesus received at His resurrection, so that we can live on earth for one thousand years, ruling and reigning with Jesus. Those who have died and been with Jesus in Heaven will be returning to the earth with Him, and they will need some kind of physical human bodies for life on the earth, but not like our sin-affected bodies that we live in now. If they were returning to where they came from, and not touching down on planet earth, they wouldn't need a physical body. Since they left this earth, they have had much better bodies where they had been living. And if Christians who are alive when He returns are headed for Heaven, they would not need to have their earthly bodies changed. They would be replaced by a heavenly body. Thus, when Paul says, "We shall all be changed in the twinkling of the eye," he must be talking about a body suited for ruling and reigning with Jesus on this earth for a thousand years. This should make even more sense as we share the prophetic significance of Christ's First Coming for His crucifixion in a later chapter.

CHAPTER THREE

IT'S ABOUT HIS COMING – NOT OUR GOING

It seems to me to be an undeniable fact that those who believe in an escape rapture are focused on the theory that Jesus is coming to rescue and remove them out of this messy world, before the start of the Great Tribulation. They are not particularly focused on the idea that Jesus is coming to rule and reign with the saints on earth. Being human, we tend to think about our current, albeit temporary, troubles. We're naturally looking for a "knight in shining armor" to deliver us from our pain and suffering. I don't blame anyone for wanting to believe this rapture scenario.

However, I believe this produces an anti-investment strategy related to Kingdom activities. Instead of preparing to rule and reign with Christ, many well-meaning Christians are preparing to escape this world. It may affect people in different ways, but I don't believe it motivates them to plan for Kingdom expansion and build Kingdom institutions. They just don't believe there is time for that. They are taught the imminence of the return of

Jesus, so they shouldn't prepare for the years and decades ahead of them.

When Brenda and I were first married and still believed in The Escape Rapture Theory, I wanted to be an evangelist and travel with just my wife. I didn't think we had time to raise children and invest in them, so they could expand God's Kingdom. I had a very short-term vision, thinking Jesus could return at any moment. After four years of marriage, while finishing seminary, I finally heard from God that we were to start a family.

Ken, our first born, is a Kingdom pioneer. He began two strategic Kingdom movements, including a Pro-Life movement, and a Patriot Church movement. We ended up with five amazing children, all gifted in unique ways, and they all have served in various ministry activities. At this point, we have fourteen incredible grandchildren, with our first great granddaughter on the way. I believe that all of them, and those who will follow them, will be used by God in one way or another. Had we continued to act on our belief that Jesus was coming any day, none of them would be here today, and God's Kingdom would have lost some amazing warriors.

People may have the rapture on their minds, but I cannot find any passage in Scripture that focuses on our being carried away to Heaven to escape the tough times that will come upon the earth. I have found plenty of passages that say Jesus is coming back to earth, but none of them talk about Him taking us to another location during the hard times. Instead, Jesus frequently warned them that they would go through tribulation, but He also assured them that He would always be with them.

It is true that God prepared an ark for Noah and his family, and He also separated the Children of Israel from the rest of Egypt when He sent the plagues. I do believe there will also be a measure of protection for those who love God during the tribulation. We shall see in coming chapters that those who are on the earth during that time will not escape to Heaven when things get nasty here.

Those who espouse the Mid-Tribulation Theory, believe the antichrist will be in power at some level until the middle of the seven years. The idea of a seven-year tribulation, divided into two parts is usually extrapolated from Daniel's seventy-weeks prophecy in Daniel 9:24-27. This passage requires a significant amount of interpretation, which is not in the scope of this book. However, it is a key passage for those who are trying to figure out the timeline of the end-time events.

Now let's examine some of the passages that talk about the "coming" of Jesus back to earth. We'll begin by returning to the most quoted rapture passages in:

1 Thessalonians:

4:13 *"But I do not want you to be ignorant, brethren, concerning those who have fallen asleep, lest you sorrow as others who have no hope.*

It's About His Coming – Not Our Going

4:14   For if we believe that Jesus died and rose again, even so God will bring with Him those who sleep in Jesus."

Clearly, this passage talks about Jesus returning to earth and bringing the dead back with Him. This fact will give them hope that they will see their dead loved ones again.

4:15   *"For this we say to you by the word of the Lord, that we who are alive and remain until THE COMING of the Lord, will by no means precede those who are asleep."*

Notice in verse 15, it's about those who remain until "THE COMING" of the Lord, not "The Going" of the saints.

4:16   *"For the Lord Himself will descend from Heaven with a shout, with the voice of an archangel, and with the trumpet of God. And the dead in Christ shall rise first.*
4:17   *Then we who are alive and remain shall be caught up together with them in the clouds to meet the Lord in the air. And thus, we shall always be with the Lord."*

Please note that in the most famous rapture verse of all, after we meet the Lord in the air, we are NOT told where we go from there. It doesn't say we will return to Heaven with Him to escape the Great Tribulation. It simply states that wherever He is, there we will be also.

The Glorious Return of King Jesus

However, as we have already shared from the passage in Matthew 24:29-31, when Jesus returns with "power and great glory," the angels "will gather together His elect from the four winds, from one end of heaven to the other." Those who are rapture believers surely must find this passage quite confusing. Here we have a gathering of the saints. For their theory to work, there must be a second gathering of the saints, because Jesus already gathered them at the rapture.

In a later chapter, we will go into more detail about the prophetic symbolism of Christ's triumphal entry into Jerusalem, before His crucifixion, but let me share a little preview now.

When Jesus came to Jerusalem for the Passover feast, according to Matthew 20:29, He came with a great multitude, including His disciples and His friends from Galilee and Jericho.

Then, we are told the following in **John 12:12-13:**

12:12	*"The next day a great multitude that had come to the feast, when they heard that Jesus was coming to Jerusalem,*
12:13	*Took branches of palm trees and went out to meet Him, and cried out: "Hosanna! Blessed is He who comes in the name of the Lord!" The King of Israel!"*

It's About His Coming – Not Our Going

Notice these important points:

1. Jesus came with a great multitude to Jerusalem for the Passover.
2. The people, in the city, heard He was coming to Jerusalem.
3. They went out of the city to MEET HIM.
4. They came back into the city with Him, proclaiming Him to be their King.
5. Jesus did not take the people from Jerusalem back to Jericho or Galilee, where He had just come from. He lodged in Bethany, an adjacent community to Jerusalem, and returned to the temple in Jerusalem in the morning to heal, teach, and pronounce judgment on the Scribes and Pharisees.

The word "meet" in the Greek has the same root word as "meet" in 1 Thessalonians 4:17. I firmly believe that Jesus Christ's coming into Jerusalem to be proclaimed "The King of the Jews" by Pilate was a type and shadow of His second coming to set up His Kingdom on the earth. More on that later, but we should take another look at the end-time passages in **Matthew 24:**

24:27   *"For as the lightning comes from the east and flashes to the west, so also will the COMING of the Son of Man be.*

24:28   *For wherever the carcass is, there the eagles will be gathered together.*

24:29   *Immediately after the tribulation of those days the sun will be darkened, and the moon will not*

24:30   *give its light; the stars will fall from heaven, and the powers of the heavens will be shaken.*
24:30   *Then the sign of the Son of Man will appear in heaven, and then all the tribes of the earth will mourn, and they will see the Son of Man COMING on the clouds of heaven with power and great glory.*
24:31   *And He will send His angels with a great sound of a trumpet, and they will gather together His elect from the four winds, from one end of heaven to the other."*

Notice- the word "COMING" in verses 27 and 30. Once again, we find no mention of anyone going straight to Heaven after we are gathered together to meet Him. Rather, the tribes of the earth mourn, because the One they refused to believe in was coming with a "Rod of Iron" (Revelation 2:27, 19:5) to cleanse the earth, like He cleansed the temple at the time of the Passover.

Now, let's look at another related passage in **Matthew 25**, which is filled with end-time parables. The first parable is about the ten virgins – five wise and five foolish.

25:6   *"And at midnight a cry was heard: Behold, the bridegroom is COMING; Go out to MEET HIM!*
25:10   *And while they went to buy, the bridegroom CAME, and those who were ready went in with him to the wedding; and the door was shut."*

It's About His Coming – Not Our Going

In this parable that Jesus told to reveal His end-time plans, we find the same word "MEET." Then we see that the bridegroom "CAME" to them, after they went out to MEET him, and they had their wedding feast there. He didn't take them away to the place he had come from to celebrate his wedding.

There are many, many other passages that talk about the COMING of Jesus. Let's look briefly at a few more in **1 Thessalonians:**

2:19   *"For what is our hope, or joy, or crown of rejoicing? Is it not even you in the presence of our Lord Jesus Christ at His COMING?*

3:13   *So that He may establish your hearts blameless in holiness before our God and Father at the COMING of our Lord Jesus Christ WITH ALL HIS SAINTS.*

5:23   *Now may the God of peace Himself sanctify you completely; and may your whole spirit, soul, and body be preserved blameless at the COMING of our Lord Jesus Christ."*

These verses confirm the focus on the return of Jesus - His COMING, and reaffirms that when He comes, it will be WITH ALL HIS SAINTS.

1 John 2:28   *"And now, little children, abide in Him, that when He appears, we may have confidence and not be ashamed before Him at His COMING.*

The Glorious Return of King Jesus

2 Peter 3:4	*And saying, "Where is the promise of His COMING? For since the fathers fell asleep, all things continue as they were from the beginning of creation.*
James 5:7-8	*Therefore be patient, brethren, until the COMING of the Lord. See how the farmer waits for the precious fruit of the earth, waiting patiently for it until it receives the early and the latter rain. You also be patient. Establish your hearts, for the COMING of the Lord is at hand."*

In the above passages, we see again that not just Jesus and Paul, but Peter, James, and John, the closest to Jesus, all talked about His COMING. They never talked about an escape rapture when He did come. Their concern was being ready for His COMING, by walking close to Him with a clear conscience.

Matthew 24:3	*"Now as He sat on the Mount of Olives, the disciples came to Him privately, saying, "Tell us, when will these things be? And what will be the sign of Your COMING, and of the end of the age?"*

This question from the disciples begins a long chapter of Jesus talking about His COMING. The word "COMING" is repeated then four more times by Jesus in Matthew 24:27, 30, 37, 39.

It's About His Coming – Not Our Going

At this point, I rest my case on this topic. I really do feel that this point is important. If the early church apostles had believed in an escape rapture, then they would have encouraged the followers of Jesus that they wouldn't have to endure great suffering. The opposite is actually true. They warned the believers that tribulation was coming, but that God would always be with them.

CHAPTER FOUR

UNANSWERED QUESTIONS IN DANIEL AND REVELATION

In this chapter, we will be dealing with some passages that are not exactly pleasant to think about. The conclusion of the matter gives us much to rejoice about and celebrate, but we must read what the prophets actually wrote, rather than treat Scripture like a "pick and choose buffet."

DANIEL

In Daniel 7, we read of Daniel's end-time visions. This chapter is filled with various beasts, including a lion with eagle's wings. My personal belief, for what it's worth, is that this represents Great Britain and America. The eagle's wings were plucked off, which would represent America's War for Independence. Then the lion was given a man's heart, representing its weakened position – no longer the powerful threat it had been militarily. I often hear people say that America is never mentioned in Scripture. I heartily disagree, because of this passage in **Daniel 7:4:**

7:4   *"The first was like a lion, and had eagle's wings. I watched till its wings were plucked off; and it was lifted up from earth and made to stand on two feet like a man, and a man's heart was given to it."*

Other beasts included a bear - probably Russia, who devoured much flesh in the days of the Soviet Union, and the leopard with four wings and four heads - possibly China. Then there was another beast, "dreadful and terrible, exceedingly strong." This beast had ten horns. Then one of the horns grew strong and replaced three of the first ten. This horn had a mouth speaking "pompous words."

The common interpretation of this unique and powerful horn is that it represents the antichrist, and thus we have a real interaction here with The Rapture Theory. Let's read a few verses from **Daniel 7** that relate directly to our study. These verses sound rather harsh, but the good news is that interspersed throughout this chapter, we have several amazing references to the courtroom of Heaven and the justice that will be meted out to those who hurt God's people.

7:21   *"I was watching, and THE SAME HORN WAS MAKING WAR AGAINST THE SAINTS, AND PREVAILING AGAINST THEM.*
7:22   *Until the Ancient of Days came, and a judgment was made in favor of the saints of the Most High,*

> and the time came for the saints to possess the kingdom.
>
> 7:24 The ten horns are ten kings who shall arise from this kingdom. And another shall rise after them; He shall be different from the first ones, and shall subdue three kings.
>
> 7:25 He shall speak pompous words against the Most High, SHALL PERSECUTE THE SAINTS OF THE MOST HIGH, and shall intend to change times and law. THEN THE SAINTS SHALL BE GIVEN INTO HIS HAND FOR A TIME AND TIMES AND HALF A TIME."

How I wish we didn't have to deal with verses 21 and 25, but it is, in fact, the inspired Word of God. This is not the only passage of this kind that we must deal with regarding end-time events. Just in case you missed it, Daniel is saying that this powerful horn would make war with the saints and prevail against them. Then he will persecute the saints of the Most High, and the saints shall be given into His hand for three and a half years, if we correctly understand the meaning of "a time, and times and half a time."

Friends, this "horn" could not war against the saints, or persecute the saints, if they had been already removed from the earth in an escape rapture. We just can't ignore these inspired verses in God's Holy Word. And we also have much more confirmation from John, the Beloved, who wrote the book of Revelation.

But before we leave **Daniel 7**, let's look at some of the positive and glorious promises from verses 9-10, 13-14 and 26-27. We are not to be fearful or defeated, because in the end we win a glorious victory.

7:9   "I watched till thrones were put in place, and the Ancient of Days was seated; His garment was white as snow, and the hair of His head was like pure wool. His throne was a fiery flame, its wheels a burning fire;

7:10   A fiery stream issued and came forth from before Him. A thousand thousands ministered to Him; Ten thousand times ten thousand stood before Him. The court was seated, and the books were opened.

7:13   I was watching in the night visions, and behold, One like the Son of Man, COMING with the clouds of heaven! He came to the Ancient of Days, and they brought Him near before Him.

7:14   Then to Him was given dominion and glory and a kingdom, that all peoples, nations, and languages should serve Him. His dominion is an everlasting dominion, which shall not pass away, and His kingdom the one which shall not be destroyed.

7:26   But the court shall be seated, and they shall take away his (the horn's) dominion, to consume and destroy it forever.

7:27   Then the kingdom and dominion, and the greatness of the kingdoms under the whole heaven, shall be given to the people, the saints of the Most High. His kingdom is an everlasting

> *kingdom, and all dominions shall serve and obey Him."*

In these passages, we see the rewards of our patience and endurance during our times of tribulation. Verse 27 declares that the saints of the Most High will be given "the Kingdom and dominion, and the greatness of the kingdoms under the whole heaven." The tables will be turned, just like when Jesus overturned the tables of the money changers in the temple. Those who had ruled before with such brutality and cruelty, will be subdued, and destroyed by Jesus. We will cover this subject a bit later in the book.

What is the obvious unanswered question about The Rapture Theory from this passage in Daniel? Simply this: How can the antichrist make war with the saints if they are up in Heaven with Jesus?

REVELATION

It's very interesting that both Daniel and Revelation deal with the time of Great Tribulation in their seventh chapters. And both Daniel and John, the writer of Revelation, fill their description with positive words of encouragement. We find the verses relevant to our study in **Revelation 7:9-17**, but we will focus on verses 9-10, 13-17.

> 7:9 *"After these things I looked, and behold, a great multitude which no one could number, of all*

	nations, tribes, peoples, and tongues, standing before the throne and before the Lamb, clothed with white robes, with palm branches in their hands,
7:10	And crying out with a loud voice, saying, 'Salvation belongs to our God who sits on the throne, and to the Lamb!'
7:13	Then one of the elders answered saying to me, 'Who are these arrayed in white robes, and where did they come from?'
7:14	And I said to him, 'Sir, you know.' So, he said to me, 'These are the ones who come out of the GREAT TRIBULATION, and washed their robes and made them white in the blood of the Lamb.'
7:15	Therefore they are before the throne of God, and serve Him day and night in His temple. And He who sits on the throne will dwell among them.
7:16	They shall neither hunger anymore nor thirst anymore; the sun shall not strike them, nor any heat;
7:17	For the Lamb who is in the midst of the throne will shepherd them and lead them to living fountains of water. And God will wipe away every tear from their eyes."

This passage is literally bursting with information about the Great Tribulation, all of which is relevant to our study. Let's point out a few important facts.

1. The people in white robes with palm branches, standing before God's throne, were so many that they could not be numbered.
2. John was told by an elder that this huge multitude came out of "the Great Tribulation."
3. These saints are given incredible favor and honor in Heaven serving in the very presence of the Most High God.
4. They have obviously suffered hunger, thirst, and the heat of the sun, but were faithful to their calling and were given white robes that were washed in the blood of the Lamb.
5. God will personally be their Shepherd and lead them to fountains of living water, never to thirst again.
6. God will wipe away every tear from their eyes.

From these six points we can confidently draw some clear conclusions:

The multitude is so enormous that they couldn't be numbered. It's hard to imagine so many believers going through the Great Tribulation if they had already been raptured to safety. We saw in Daniel 7 that this was not the case. It was the saints that were persecuted. To presume that so many people were converted after the rapture, is another major stretch, in my opinion.

We are told that these people suffered from hunger, thirst, and the elements. This does make sense if they had lived through a time when they couldn't buy or sell, because they wouldn't receive the "mark." If they couldn't do any commerce, then they couldn't own property or buy food and water in a grocery store.

We have seen a bit of a mild tribulation preview with the Covid-19 vaccine mandates on a world-wide scale. Many lost their jobs and access to their bank accounts. Some were taken to quarantine centers, where they were held like prisoners. Travel freedom was severely restricted, and globalist leaders are still trying to extend or perpetuate this means of controlling the population.

On the other hand, those who faithfully endured the Great Tribulation received incredible, eternal rewards. In fact, Revelation 12:11 declares that they actually overcame the evil one by the blood of the Lamb, the word of their testimony, and by loving not their own lives, even unto death.

As part of their great reward, they experienced a Heavenly version of Psalm 23. The Great Shepherd leads them to "living fountains of water and will wipe away every tear from their eyes."

What then is the obvious unanswered question related to this passage in Revelation 7? It is this: How can there be this huge number of saints, more than could be numbered, who went through suffering in the Tribulation, if all the believers were raptured before the persecution of the antichrist began?

CHAPTER FIVE

THE RESTRAINING – WHO IS TAKEN OUT OF THE WAY?

One of the commonly used Scripture passages used to justify The Escape Rapture Theory is 2 Thessalonians 2:1-12. This passage is about the second COMING of Jesus and the work and exposure of the antichrist. Most rapture theorists maintain that these verses are saying that the Holy Spirit will be taken away from the earth, along with all the saints, so that the antichrist can be revealed and do his evil deeds.

However, this passage is extremely unclear as to what it is actually saying and is subject to gross misinterpretation. In verse 2:7, in the Greek text, we have the use of the pronoun "he" twice, without any clarity as to whom each "he" is referring to. Let's read the text, as translated by the NKJV scholars, and then take a closer look at what this passage could actually mean.

The Restraining – Who is Taken Out of the Way?

2 Thessalonians 2:1-12:

2:1 "Now, brethren, concerning the COMING of our Lord Jesus Christ and our gathering together to Him, we ask you,

2:2 Not to be soon shaken in mind or troubled, either by spirit or by word or by letter, as if from us, as though the day of Christ had come.

2:3 Let no one deceive you by any means; <u>for that Day will not come</u> unless the falling away comes first, and the man of sin is revealed, the son of perdition,

2:4 Who opposes and exalts himself above all that is called God or that is worshiped, so that he sits as God in the temple of God, showing himself that he is God.

2:5 Do you not remember that when I was still with you, I told you these things?

2:6 And now you know what is restraining, that he may be revealed in his own time.

2:7 For the mystery of lawlessness is already at work; only He who now restrains <u>will do so</u> until He is taken out of the way.

2:8 And then the lawless one will be revealed, whom the Lord will consume with the breath of His mouth and destroy with the brightness of His coming.

2:9 The coming of the lawless one is according to the working of Satan, with all power, signs and lying wonders

The Glorious Return of King Jesus

2:10   And with all unrighteous deception among those who perish, because they did not receive the love of the truth, that they might be saved.
2:11   And for this reason, God will send them strong delusion, that they should believe the lie,
2:12   That they all may be condemned who did not believe the truth but had pleasure in unrighteousness."

NOTE: In verse 2:7, the word "He" is capitalized twice, indicating the translators believed that it referred to God, or Jesus, or the Holy Spirit. Also note that several words in verses 2:3 and 2:7 are in italics in the Bible (underlined for clarity here), which indicates they are not in the Greek text, but are inserted to help the passage make sense.

If only we had a recording of what Paul told the Thessalonians when he was with them. He says in verse 2:6, *"And now you know what is restraining, that he may be revealed in his own time."* Since we didn't hear what Paul told them in person, we can only speculate what he actually said. However, the context of the previous verses gives us a very strong indication of what Paul really meant.

At this point, we should examine the Greek word for "revealed." The English transliteration is "apokaloopto." It means "to take off the cover, to expose." The implication is that what is in the pot has been hidden. But now we're taking the lid off and discovering what's been cooking, and we didn't even realize what was there. This revealing can be of something evil, but it can also be of

The Restraining – Who is Taken Out of the Way?

something good or wonderful, such as revealing to a Jew that Jesus is his or her Messiah. This could be very significant in our understanding of verses 2:6-8.

Another important word in this passage is the word for "restrain." The Greek word is "Katecho." This means to "hold down or hold fast." This is the opposite of lifting the lid. It's about holding it down, so something cannot be revealed or exposed. This understanding should open up a fresh and more accurate interpretation of this mysterious passage.

Now, let's take a look at an alternate interpretation, which does support a non-pretribulation rapture theory:

Verse 2:6 *"And now you know what is restraining, that he may be revealed in his own time."*

I believe both the "he" and the "his" in this verse actually refer to Jesus and His return. The chapter begins with "the COMING of the Lord Jesus Christ and our gathering together to Him." The revealing refers to Jesus coming in the clouds with power and great glory where every eye will see Him. This would clearly be a revealing. Suddenly, everyone will see that Jesus is King of kings and Lord of lords.

So, what would then be restraining or "holding down" that revealing? It would be the fact, as Paul just mentioned, that Jesus Himself wouldn't return until the antichrist had come. It makes total sense to me, and this is my understanding of what Paul is clearly saying: "Don't believe reports that Jesus has already come (the "Day of Christ"), because that day can't come until the antichrist has been exposed and 'taken out of the way' by the COMING of Christ."

The restraining then is obviously the fact that the antichrist has not yet come, which would be consistent with the phrase "what is restraining" in verse 2:6. The "what" is the coming of the antichrist. However, we must also deal with verse 2:7, which says, *"He who now restrains will do so, until he be taken out of the way."*

At this point, it's not the "what" that is restraining, but the "He" who does the restraining. Probably, the best interpretation would be that the first "He" refers to God. He is restraining, or holding back, the return of Jesus. Acts 3:21 says the Heavens must receive Jesus until the time of the restitution of all things. God has to restrain Jesus from returning to earth until all has been fulfilled.

The second "he" would have to refer to the antichrist, who will be dealt with and exposed by the "brightness" of Jesus' COMING. It should be translated as "he" in lower case, since it refers to the antichrist being exposed, not Jesus or the Holy Spirit. The Rapture Theory puts forth that it's the Holy Spirit who is taken out of the way, but Paul didn't even mention the Holy Spirit in this chapter. He only talks about the return of Jesus and the work of the antichrist.

The Restraining – Who is Taken Out of the Way?

When a writer uses a pronoun, it always refers back to the noun - the antecedent. The "he" must refer back to someone who has already been talked about in a previous sentence. In this passage, the "he" should refer either to Jesus or to the antichrist. Grammatically, it could not refer to the Holy Spirit.

Next, let's follow up with verse 2:8, which starts with the words "And then." The adverb "then" is very significant. In the Greek, it doesn't mean "after this," it means "at the time of."

We could translate verse 2:8 like this:

And then (at that same time) the *lawless one* will be revealed, whom the Lord will consume with the breath of His mouth and destroy with the brightness of His coming.

In other words, the antichrist will be exposed by and "taken out of the way" by the coming of Jesus when He returns to the earth. It will be not to remove us, and the Holy Spirit, from the earth, but to judge the earth and set up His Kingdom, with us at His side, ruling and reigning with Him.

I apologize to the reader if this still seems confusing. Personally, I don't believe the thesis of this book depends on this chapter. However, for me, it now makes sense. I am satisfied that the passage we're dealing with does not imply the removal of the church or the Holy Spirit from the earth. Of course, this is totally consistent with the other passages which we have dealt with to this point.

There are two other passages that Pre-Tribulation Rapture theorists use to support their theory. We will investigate these in the following chapter.

CHAPTER SIX

NOT APPOINTED TO WRATH AND THE OPEN DOOR

It's now time to deal with two other arguments that are often used to support The Escape Rapture Theory.

ESCAPING THE WRATH

The most frequently quoted verses used to support this argument are found in **1 Thessalonians 5:9-11:**

5:9 *"For God did not appoint us to wrath, but to obtain salvation through our Lord Jesus Christ,*
5:10 *Who died for us, that whether we wake or sleep, we should live together with Him.*
5:11 *Therefore comfort one another and edify one another, just as you also are doing."*

The only words in this passage that are frequently quoted are the first eight words: "For God did not appoint us to wrath."

The argument goes like this: God won't let us go through the Great Tribulation, because He did not appoint us to wrath. They mistakenly equate the word "wrath" with the Great Tribulation. However, it takes very little examination of how this word is used to discover that the word "wrath" is not about the tribulation, but rather the judgment of the wicked who have rebelliously walked away from God.

The first clue is in the second part of verse 5:9. Instead of being appointed to wrath, we are appointed to salvation through our Lord Jesus Christ. Verse 5:10 amplifies the meaning of that salvation. Because of His death, His salvation envelopes us at all times. Therefore, the idea that salvation means escaping the tribulation is not logical or reasonable. Paul is clearly talking about being saved from God's judgment through His sacrifice on the cross. To some, verse 5:11 means that they should comfort one another because they won't have to go through tribulation. It actually means to comfort one another whenever they do go through tribulation, because God promises He will always be with us. Jesus had frequently warned His disciples that they would be persecuted and possibly die as martyrs. His comfort was that He would be with them through it all.

When the Bible speaks about God's wrath, it's almost always regarding the judgment of the wicked, rather than persecution or tribulation. So many other Scriptures support this fact:

Not Appointed to Wrath and the Open Door

John 3:36	"He who believes in the Son has everlasting life; and he who does not believe in the Son shall not see life, but the WRATH of God abides on him.
Romans 1:18	For the WRATH of God is revealed from Heaven against all ungodliness and unrighteousness of men, who suppress the truth in unrighteousness.
Romans 2:5	But in accordance with your hardness and your impenitent heart you are treasuring up for yourself WRATH in the day of WRATH and revelation of the righteous judgment of God.
Romans 5:9	Much more then, having now been justified by His blood, we shall be saved from WRATH through Him.
1 Thessalonians 1:10	And to wait for His Son from heaven, whom He raised from the dead, even Jesus who delivers us from the WRATH to come.
1 Thessalonians 2:16	Forbidding us to speak to the Gentiles that they might be saved, so as always to fill up the measure of their sins; but WRATH has come upon them, to the uttermost.

The Glorious Return of King Jesus

Matthew 3:7b   *Brood of vipers! Who warned you to flee from the WRATH to come?*

Luke 21:23   *But woe to those who are pregnant and to those who are nursing babies in those days! For there will be great distress in the land, and WRATH upon this people."*

This Luke 21:23 passage could be interpreted as wrath being a part of persecution and tribulation. However, it clearly speaks about the destruction of Jerusalem that took place in 70 A.D. under the Roman General Titus. This was specifically God's judgment against a nation who had rejected their Messiah. It's not about God's final judgment at the end of days.

NOTE: At this point, we should mention for those devoted students of eschatology, that a significant number of scholars and teachers believe that the Great Tribulation has already taken place. The Jews endured terrible suffering in 70 A.D.; therefore, the Great Tribulation applies to the nation of Israel and not the end-time church. However, we find some significant problems with this theory as well.

This is the Preterite position, as defined in the Preface. Perhaps the biggest problem with this theory is a multitude that no man could number, who had been through great tribulation, is described in Revelation 7:9-14. The number of people killed in and around Jerusalem,

Not Appointed to Wrath and the Open Door

including Masada, would not even come close to that description.

Another problem with that theory is in the **Matthew 24:29-30**:

24:29   *"Immediately after the tribulation of those days the sun will be darkened, and the moon will not give its light; the stars will fall from heaven, and the powers of the heavens will be shaken.*
24:30   *Then the sign of the Son of Man will appear in heaven, and then all the tribes of the earth will mourn, and they will see the Son of Man coming on the clouds of heaven with power and great glory."*

I looked up the word "immediately" and it means "immediately" or "at once." Since it's in the Greek text, and it's the inspired Word of God, I can't ignore it.

Let's quote a few more verses, containing the word "wrath."

Ephesians 2:3   "Among whom also we all once conducted ourselves in the lusts of our flesh, fulfilling the desires of the flesh and of the mind, and were by nature children of WRATH, just as the others.
Ephesians 5:6   Let no one deceive you with empty words, for because of these things

The Glorious Return of King Jesus

	the WRATH of God comes upon the sons of disobedience.
Colossians 3:6	Because of these things the WRATH of God is coming upon the sons of disobedience."

There are twelve references in the book of Revelation that contain the word WRATH. Eleven of these talk about the WRATH of God. The other reference is found in Revelation 12:12, and it describes the WRATH of the devil, who knows his time is short.

In summary, we can say that the uses of the term "WRATH" in Revelation are typical of the whole Bible. The word "wrath" is used with very few exceptions to talk about the judgment of the wicked, rather than the tribulation brought about by the antichrist.

Throughout the entire history of the church, when the church was in relationship with Jesus and not just a religion, Christians have suffered persecution. We have been told that there have been more martyrs in recent times than in early church history. Millions in countries controlled by communists or false religions have been severely persecuted and/or executed for their faith in Christ. Many had been taught they would escape the tribulation, but they have experienced unimaginable suffering. Most of us in the West have been blessed with extended periods of peace in our lifetimes, but much of the world has not been so fortunate.

Not Appointed to Wrath and the Open Door

Corrie ten Boom's family loved God and cared about the suffering of the Jewish people. They hid many Jews from the Nazis, until the family was betrayed and then arrested for their acts of kindness. Corrie and her sister Betsie were sent to a German concentration camp. The women there underwent some of the worst suffering in the history of the church at the hands of the Nazis. Corrie's beloved sister, Betsie, died in the camp before the time of liberation. After experiencing such horrific suffering there, Corrie fought against the teaching that Christians would be raptured to escape the Great Tribulation; it brought real harm and confusion to believers and should not be taught.

Let me quote a portion of a letter Corrie wrote in 1974, as published by One Thing Ministries:

"There are some among us teaching there will be no tribulation, that the Christians will be able to escape all this. These are the false teachers that Jesus was warning us to expect in the latter days. Most of them have little knowledge of what is already going on across the world. I have been in countries where the saints are already suffering terrible persecution."

"In China, the Christians were told, 'Don't worry, before the tribulation comes you will be translated - raptured.' Then came a terrible persecution. Millions of Christians were tortured to death."

"Corrie then quotes a Chinese bishop, who stated, 'We have failed. We should have made the people strong for

persecution rather than telling them Jesus would come first. Tell the people how to be strong in times of persecution, how to stand when the tribulation comes - to stand and not faint.'"

To teach people who are suffering in third-world countries that they will escape the Great Tribulation is meaningless to them. They have already experienced considerable and inconceivable persecution on an ongoing basis. Instead, they need to be strengthened in their spirit to be strong and courageous and to love not their lives unto death.

This sounds harsh and frightening to us as Westerners, but there is so much good news that we will share later in this book.

The most important thing to remember is the promise of Jesus:

Matthew 28:20   *"Lo, I am with you always, even to the end of the age."*

He will still be our Great Shepherd, and like David said:

Psalm 23:4-6   *"Yea, though I walk through the valley of the shadow of death, I will fear no evil; for You are with me; You prepare a table before me in the presence of my enemies. You anoint my head with oil; my cup runs over. Surely goodness and mercy shall follow me all the days of my life; and I*

> will dwell in the house of the Lord forever."

If He is with me, I have no reason to fear. He will strengthen us, guide us, comfort us, and reward us throughout eternity for anything we suffer for Him. We can truly trust Him in every circumstance. Remember the last two verses of Psalm 23. I see these as the reward for walking with Him through that valley. The rewards in a nutshell are great honor, fresh anointing, abundance of provision and an eternal home in His presence. Sounds great to me!

THE OPEN DOOR

Another passage frequently used to defend The Escape Rapture Theory is:

Revelation 4:1   "After these things I looked, and behold, a door standing open in Heaven. And the voice which I heard was like a trumpet speaking with me, saying, 'Come up here, and I will show you things which must take place after this.'"

For the rapture theorists, this verse is like a secret code. It not only describes a visit to Heaven by John the Beloved, but it's also an invitation for all to come up to Heaven in the rapture, while judgment occurs on earth for those "left behind." In my humble opinion, this is a huge stretch.

The Glorious Return of King Jesus

However, it is one of the very few passages in Revelation that could possibly refer to an escape from the Great Tribulation.

However, there is nothing in this verse, or the verses following, indicating that anyone, other than John, was invited to Heaven to see what God is going to do in the latter days. He was simply given a Heavenly encounter, similar to what Paul had experienced and shared in 2 Corinthians 12.

In the first three chapters of Revelation, we have the introduction and the letters to the seven churches of Asia Minor. Chapter four is the beginning of the end-time prophecies. John was taken up to Heaven where he received the revelation of what was to come, not to escape the tribulation. Even John experienced persecution. Church tradition tells us that they tried to boil him in oil, but they were unable able to kill him, so he was exiled to the island of Patmos. John was a prisoner in exile when he had this supernatural experience, which he recorded in the book called "Revelation."

To sum up this chapter, I believe the most important point is this: We are told The Rapture will come before The Great Tribulation because "we are not appointed to wrath." However, 1 Thessalonians 5:9 is clearly talking about God's final judgment on sin, not a time of tribulation. Nevertheless, this verse is always quoted in defense of The Escape Rapture Theory.

Not Appointed to Wrath and the Open Door

Both the 1 Thessalonians 5:9 and the Revelation 4:1 "open door" passages, have no real merit as arguments for The Escape Rapture Theory and do not pass even the basic minimum standards of hermeneutics - how to interpret Scripture. If we are honest with ourselves, we must admit that these are very weak arguments and signs of grasping at straws to support a weak theory.

But let's move on now to what I believe is a very significant insight that will give us hope and confidence in the wonderful future and destiny we will experience in the days and endless age to come.

CHAPTER SEVEN

A POWERFUL PROPHETIC TYPE AND SHADOW

This chapter is one that I have been looking forward to writing, although what I am about to share is not a "Thus-saith-the-Lord" proof. However, I do feel strongly that it was given to me as an insight or revelation. A brief preview was shared in a previous chapter. Since then, I have been studying the book of Matthew, as well as the other gospels, and I believe God has given me more insight concerning this revelation.

THE THESIS:

Almost everything that took place when Jesus came from Galilee to Jerusalem where He was crucified, was a type and shadow of what will happen when He returns to earth again. Consequently, I'm convinced that the open-minded reader will find the parallels quite stunning and convincing. Here's the condensed version, which we will expand upon in this chapter:

A Powerful Prophetic Type and Shadow

Jesus left Galilee, His primary home, along with His disciples and a great multitude of followers. He healed the sick and taught the people on the journey first to Jericho and then on to Jerusalem for the Passover Feast. It was now His appointed time to become the Passover Lamb, as a sacrifice for all of our sins, as prophesied by John the Baptist in John 1:29, 35.

As Jesus approached Jerusalem, a great multitude accompanied Him. He sent His disciples ahead to get the colt of a donkey for Him to ride. Hearing of His coming, another great multitude came out of the city to meet Him. Then they ushered Jesus into the city with a great coronation parade which included waving palm branches and proclaiming Him the King of Israel.

Upon arriving at the temple, the first thing Jesus did was overthrow the tables of the money changers. He proclaimed that His Father's house was to be called a House of Prayer, while they had made it a "den of thieves." Then He healed the sick and taught the people during the week before the Passover. During this time, Jesus spent much time pronouncing judgment on the Scribes and Pharisees, condemning them for their hypocrisy and wicked hearts.

Jesus and His disciples spent the night in Bethany, basically a suburb of Jerusalem, but returned to Jerusalem to teach in the temple during the day. It was then time for the Last Supper with His disciples before the Passover.

The Glorious Return of King Jesus

After His arrest, Jesus was given a mock coronation ceremony, which included being given a royal robe by Herod's men and a scarlet robe by the Roman soldiers. Then a crown of thorns was cruelly placed on His head by the soldiers.

The final part of His "First Coming" coronation was nailing Him on a Roman cross, which was His throne, and placing a sign over His head that read, "This is Jesus, the King of the Jews."

These events were all a prophetic picture of what will happen at the "Second Coming" of Jesus:

- He will return with a host of saints from His home in Heaven.
- He will be ushered into Jerusalem with a glorious parade.
- He will bring judgment and justice, taking the wicked to court and sentencing them to hell.
- He will also heal the sick and wipe away all tears from sad eyes.
- He will then have the "First Supper" of His Kingdom on the earth, the "Marriage Supper of the Lamb."
- Finally, there will be a coronation ceremony where He is crowned and placed on His throne, with His Bride at His side.

We will cover more details now, as we proceed to unwrap this story. It's an adventure I've been waiting for!

A Powerful Prophetic Type and Shadow

ORIGIN OF JESUS' JOURNEY

Jesus was born in Bethlehem because He was a descendent of David. After his time in Egypt, He grew up in Nazareth, a city of Galilee. He met many of His disciples there, and it's where much of His ministry time was spent. He was known by many as "Jesus of Nazareth." For our purposes, in comparing His first and second comings to Jerusalem, we'll say that Galilee was His home 2000 years ago, as Heaven is now His home.

As we follow Matthew's account:

Matthew 19:1	"He departed from Galilee and came to the region of Judea beyond the Jordan.
Matthew 19:2	And great multitudes followed Him, and He healed them there."

We notice this phenomenon of "great multitudes" at every stage of His journey, which is symbolic of Jesus returning to earth with a great multitude of saints. Another event that occurred at each stage of His journey, was the interrogation of Jesus by the Pharisees. This has no parallel with His Second Coming, but it is typically what happens when the religious people of today hear about a revival that doesn't match their expectations. Rather than rejoice that their Messiah had visited them, they saw Jesus as a threat to their control over the people and sought to destroy Him.

The Glorious Return of King Jesus

THE JOURNEY CONTINUES

Please notice what happens now on this journey. Its significance will be seen shortly.

Matthew 20:29-34:

20:29   "Now as they went out of Jericho, a great multitude followed Him.
20:30   And behold, two blind men sitting by the road, when they heard that Jesus was passing by, cried out, saying, 'Have mercy on us, O Lord, Son of David!'
20:31   Then the multitude warned them that they should be quiet, but they cried out all the more, saying, 'Have mercy on us, O Lord, Son of David!'
20:32   So Jesus stood still and called them, and said, 'What do you want Me to do for you?'
20:33   They said to Him, 'Lord, that our eyes might be opened.'
20:34   So Jesus had compassion and touched their eyes. And immediately their eyes received sight, and they followed Him."

When Jesus asked the blind men what they wanted Him to do for them, He obviously knew they wanted to be able to see. They knew they were blind, and they didn't try to hide it. They were desperate for a miracle and knew that Jesus was the Son of David, and not just "Jesus of Nazareth," as others called Him. The fact is that they

A Powerful Prophetic Type and Shadow

already had clearer vision than another group, which Jesus addresses later in Jerusalem, who wouldn't acknowledge their own blindness.

ON TO JERUSALEM

To fulfill prophecy and to foretell His Second Coming, Jesus instructed His disciples to arrange for His mode of transportation into Jerusalem. It wasn't a chariot or a horse-drawn carriage.

Matthew 21:1-5 gives us part of the story:

21:1	"Now when they drew near Jerusalem, and came to Bethphage, at the Mount of Olives, then Jesus sent two disciples,
21:2	Saying to them, 'Go into the village opposite you, and immediately you will find a donkey tied, and a colt with her. Loose them and bring them to Me.'
22:3	'And if anyone says anything to you, you shall say, The Lord has need of them.' And immediately he will send them.
22:4	All this was done that it might be fulfilled which was spoken by the prophet, saying:
22:5	Tell the daughter of Zion. 'Behold, your King is coming to you, Lowly, and sitting on a donkey, a colt, the foal of a donkey.'"

As has been often taught, the First Coming of Christ was as the Lamb of God, whereas His Second Coming will be as the Lion of the Tribe of Judah. His First Coming was with the most humble beginning, being born in a Bethlehem stable and laid in a manger. His Second Coming will manifest His Heavenly Glory and Eternal Majesty.

His First Coming into the City of Jerusalem was on the colt of a donkey. The gospel of Mark tells us this colt had never been ridden before. Obviously, for Jesus to ride this colt was miraculous, but I find it easy to believe that this colt recognized his Creator just like Balaam's donkey recognized the angel standing in his way. The Second Coming of Jesus will be on a celestial white horse, and every eye will see Him in resplendent majesty (Revelation 19:20).

For the next significant part of the story, we go to **John 12:12-13:**

12:12   "The next day A GREAT MULTITUDE that had come to the feast, when they heard that Jesus was coming to Jerusalem,
12:13   Took branches of palm trees and went out to MEET HIM, and cried out: 'Hosanna! Blessed is He who comes in the name of the Lord! The King of Israel.'"

This is the perfect type and shadow of Jesus' Second Coming, because it was a GREAT MULTITUDE of people who came out to MEET Jesus and usher Him into the city. He didn't come to take them back to Galilee with Him. He came to be crowned their King on the cross. Again, we

A Powerful Prophetic Type and Shadow

remind the reader that the word "MEET" here has the same root word as the word "MEET" in **1 Thessalonians 4:17:**

4:17 "Then we who are alive and remain shall be caught up together with them in the clouds to MEET the Lord in the air. And thus we shall always be with the Lord."

As I meditated on these passages about Jesus coming into Jerusalem, I have seen a number of things that I had never noticed before. Because the people were there for the feast, many tribes and regions of the world were represented. And we know there is going to be a great feast at some point that we call "The Marriage Supper of the Lamb." But Jesus also compares His return to the coming of a Bridegroom for His Bride in Matthew 25. My thoughts on this are that the coming Marriage Feast could take place on the earth before an actual Coronation Ceremony. This would legally enable the Bride of Christ to officially reign with Jesus as His Queen. We'll see a bit later how this could fit into God's plans.

At any rate, we have seen that the Scripture talks about a GREAT MULTITUDE that followed Jesus from Galilee and Jericho. And now we read about another GREAT MULTITUDE coming out of Jerusalem to MEET Jesus as He approaches the city. In my mind and understanding, it's a perfect picture of the SECOND COMING.

Jesus will come with all the saints from Heaven, then those who are still alive will rise to MEET Jesus and the saints in the air. All will be given resurrected bodies at that time. Then we will all join together in the greatest coronation parade in the history of the world, proclaiming Jesus the King of kings and Lord of lords. It will indeed be incredibly glorious!

THE FIRST EVENT ON JESUS' AGENDA - CLEANSING THE TEMPLE

Matthew 21:12-13 describes the cleansing of the temple:

21:12 *"Then Jesus went into the temple of God and drove out all those who bought and sold in the temple, and overturned the tables of the money changers and the seats of those who sold doves.*
21:13 *And He said to them, 'It is written, My house shall be called a house of prayer,' but you have made it a 'den of thieves.'"*

If Jesus' FIRST COMING foretells His SECOND COMING, then we may see Him first focus on religious organizations and ministries that have merchandized the gospel. He's not necessarily condemning them to hell, but He is stopping their way of doing business, bringing discipline and purity or holiness to His Kingdom. It may also be prophetic of His judgment on the globalist billionaires who are aligned with the antichrist.

A Powerful Prophetic Type and Shadow

Following this temple cleansing episode, we are told that the blind and the lame came to Jesus, obviously not deterred by what they had seen Him do. Jesus immediately began to heal them, but this was not what the religious leaders wanted. The Pharisees approached Jesus and "were indignant" (Matthew 21:15). What seemingly bothered them the most was the fact that the children were crying out in the temple saying, "Hosanna to the Son of David!"

The religious spirit in the Pharisees feared one thing more than any other. They feared that the people would believe in Jesus as their Messiah, which would totally mess with their elite status and completely remove their power over the people in Israel. Today, the religious spirit still fights every move of God, such as the revival/awakening that is happening on university campuses across this nation, as I write this chapter. Religious leaders hate allowing the common people to take the lead and bypass them. Like the Pharisees, they believe God would only use them to start a revival, because they are the most educated and have seniority in the Kingdom. But Paul reminds us, in 1 Corinthians 1, that God has chosen the "nobodies" and the "foolish" people in this world to confound those who think they are the wise "somebodies" in society.

THE FIG TREE

According to Matthew 21:17, Jesus spent the night in Bethany. Luke says Jesus went to the Mount of Olives and spent the night there (Luke 21:7). It sounds like a contradiction, but the fact is that they are virtually in the same place. Bethany was located next to the Mount of Olives, so Luke is obviously speaking of the larger territory where Bethany was located. In the morning, Jesus was returning to Jerusalem, and He saw a fig tree along the way. Being hungry, He looked for fruit on it. Finding nothing but leaves, He cursed the fig tree and it immediately withered away. Jesus used this incident primarily to teach His disciples the authority they held if they only had the faith to believe.

However, we also can see a very significant prophetic application here. This fig tree was alive with healthy green leaves, but it had not yet produced fruit. Jesus was surely warning His disciples that He expected them to abide in Him, as He taught them in John 15, so they could produce fruit for Him to enjoy. And in respect to His SECOND COMING, I believe that Jesus will actually shut down ministries that just look good from a distance. They are not producing any fruit, because they are obviously not abiding in Him - the Vine.

One more interesting detail, Bethany means "House of Figs." It was known for its figs, but this tree was not producing the fruit it should have. It reminds me of the story of Ruth. Elimelech and Naomi lived in Bethlehem, which means "House of Bread." Sadly, there was no bread in the House of Bread, so they moved to Moab to get bread from foreigners. Later, after losing her husband and two sons, Naomi heard there was bread again in the House of Bread, and she returned with her daughter-in-law Ruth. I believe that story is prophetic for our day. Many people left the church because they weren't being fed the Bread of Life. However, God is reviving His church and fresh bread is once again being made in His House. Many of those who have left the church will return and those who were not believers before will come with them.

ATTACKS FROM THE CHIEF PRIESTS AND ELDERS

When Jesus returned to the temple (Matthew 21:23), He began teaching the people again. The chief priests and elders obviously thought Jesus should have asked their permission to teach and heal the sick in the temple, and they confronted Him about His authority to do these things. Jesus responded with a question of His own, which they couldn't answer. Then He began to talk to them in parables, which clearly condemned them for rejecting the Son of God. The Pharisees and Sadducees also asked Him questions, trying to trap Jesus in His theology. He continued to diffuse every attack with an anointed answer that left them speechless.

JESUS PRONOUNCES JUDGEMENT ON SCRIBES AND PHARISEES

Before beginning this book, I had never paid much attention to Matthew 23, although I had read it dozens of times. Today, I see it as incredibly important and so prophetic of what Jesus will do in His SECOND COMING. Jesus turned from talking to the Scribes and Pharisees and began talking to the multitude and His disciples.

I now see Matthew 23 as a courtroom session where the Judge of all the earth is sentencing those that He brought to trial, as mentioned frequently in Daniel 7. The "multitude" and His disciples are the witnesses in the courtroom. I find this quite amazing.

INITIAL CHARGES AGAINST THE SCRIBES AND PHARISEES

Jesus begins by listing their offenses and violations of God's law. He mentions the fact that they put heavy burdens on people that they themselves don't carry. They do everything to bolster their own status and to be seen by men. They love the luxuries and benefits that their titles give them, including the best seats at the synagogues and feasts. They love the honored greetings in the marketplace and the titles they carry such as "Rabbi."

Jesus then warns His followers to avoid being like them. He challenges them to avoid all pride and selfish ambition and reminds them that the proud will be humbled, and the humble will be exalted in His Kingdom.

THE "WOES"

Jesus continues to accuse and pronounce judgment on the Scribes and Pharisees. He used the word "WOE" eight times in Matthew 23. With each "woe" came an accusation of evil actions due to their proud and evil hearts, plus an actual verdict with a sentence of punishment.

A Powerful Prophetic Type and Shadow

HYPOCRISY

In this chapter and the previous chapter, Jesus calls these religious/political leaders HYPOCRITES eight times. Jesus amplifies the fact that they like to look spiritual, but they are guilty of things like stealing from widows and praying long prayers to make themselves look good.

FOOLS AND BLIND

Jesus continues to indict these leaders by calling them FOOLS twice and BLIND five times. Remember the two blind men who knew they were blind? Jesus healed them near Jericho on the way to Jerusalem. Jesus had them say the obvious, because He wanted an oral admission that they acknowledged their blindness and wanted sight. The religious leaders wouldn't think of admitting they were blind; thus, their spiritual vision wasn't eligible for a healing touch. Sadly, we see some similar attitudes in many of our theologians and church leaders. I want to be on record that I do recognize my blindness in many areas. I pray the song, "Open my eyes, Lord, I want to see Jesus."

SERPENTS AND A BROOD OF VIPERS RECEIVE THEIR SENTENCE FROM THE JUDGE

Jesus showed no mercy or diplomacy in talking to or about these leaders. He wasn't in the business of trying to compromise with them in any way. He knew their hearts and whom they served. He pronounces judgment on them with the strongest language yet calling them, "Serpents, brood of vipers. How can you escape the condemnation of hell?" This was their sentence from the Judge of all the earth.

COMPARIBLE JUDGMENT WITH THE SECOND COMING

As I meditate on the end-time possibilities, comparing the FIRST COMING with the SECOND COMING, I am persuaded that even as Jesus spent a few days between the Triumphal Entry Parade and the crucifixion, He will take time to accomplish similar things before His glorious coronation, as King of kings and Lord of lords. The first thing on His agenda was cleansing the temple and pronouncing judgment on the evil rulers of His day. Remember that the chief priests, the Scribes, and the Pharisees, were not only the religious leaders; they were also clearly the political leaders. They controlled most of the economic and political decisions, albeit with the Romans overseeing them.

Jesus first dealt with those who were in it for profit when He overthrew the money changers. Then He pronounced judgment on the religious leaders, taking them to court and actually sentencing them to hell. I am expecting Jesus to do something similar at His SECOND COMING. He will judge the political and religious leaders who have lived in luxury off the donations of the oppressed and built their own little "kingdoms," rather than building His. He will also judge the globalist financial leaders who have made trillions of dollars robbing the poor and working class.

A Powerful Prophetic Type and Shadow

Let's look at the prophetic Scriptures that speak of these things. **Matthew 24** is a great place to start. Let's read a portion and compare it to **Revelation 19.**

Matthew 24:27	"For as the lightning comes from the east and flashes to the west, so also will the coming of the Son of Man be.
Matthew 24:28	For wherever the carcass is, there the eagles will be gathered together."
Revelation 19:17-18	"Then I saw an angel standing in the sun; and he cried with a loud voice, saying to all the birds that fly in the midst of heaven, 'Come and gather together for the supper of the great God, that you may eat the flesh of kings, the flesh of captains, the flesh of mighty men, the flesh of horses and of those who sit on them, and the flesh of all people, free and slave, both small and great.'
Revelation 19:21	And the rest were killed with the sword which proceeded from the mouth of Him who sat on the horse. And all the birds were filled with their flesh."

Matthew 24:27-28 clearly tie in this judgment on His enemies and the enemies of Israel with Jesus' SECOND COMING. The judgment produces a feast for the eagles or vultures that eat the meat of dead animals and, in this case, humans. The passage in Revelation 19:17, 21 refers to the birds feasting on the slain, when Jesus comes in power and great glory. The first thing Jesus does is judge the wicked who follow the antichrist. Some may say these are two separate events, but I find that quite a stretch when there are so many similarities in the entire story.

THE DAYS OF NOAH

We shared in Chapter One of this book two verses that included "one taken and the other left." These verses have been seriously misinterpreted (Matthew 24:40-41). What needs to be mentioned here is that when Jesus comes, judgment will be on the earth for those who are "taken" like the people in Noah's day who were "taken" away in the flood. I don't want to be taken. That actually means being punished by God, and it will happen without warning.

THE DANIEL PROPHECY

Daniel's end-time prophecies are probably the most difficult to interpret. We find the same things repeated a number of times, causing many of the events to not be in chronological order. What I love about Daniel and his prophecies is the three-fold repetition in Daniel 7 with the

A Powerful Prophetic Type and Shadow

encouraging word that the "Saints shall possess the Kingdom."

One passage in Daniel, which we have failed to refer to, is another description of Jesus' SECOND COMING. Let's look at it in **Daniel 7:13-14:**

7:13 *"I was watching in the night visions, and behold, One like the Son of Man, COMING IN THE CLOUDS OF HEAVEN! He came to the Ancient of Days, and they brought Him near before Him.*
7:14 *Then to Him was given dominion and glory and a kingdom, that all peoples, nations, and languages should serve Him. His dominion is an everlasting dominion, which shall not pass away, and His kingdom, the one which shall not be destroyed."*

What a beautiful picture of a glorious ceremony, where God the Father (the Ancient of Days) presents to Jesus (The Son of Man) all dominion and glory and a kingdom. An everlasting Kingdom is established at the beginning of His one-thousand-year reign of peace on earth that will not be destroyed!

THE LAST SUPPER AND THE MARRIAGE SUPPER OF THE LAMB

Before Jesus gave Himself up to be crucified, He had one last meal with His disciples, known as "The Last Supper."

The Glorious Return of King Jesus

This event seems to be prophetic of what is coming - "The Marriage Supper of the Lamb."

I believe, as I've taught in previous books, that Jesus shared with His disciples what He was giving them. He was transferring miraculous giftings that manifested through His body as the bread, and the anointing and cleansing power of the Holy Spirit, as represented by the wine. However, it was also a very significant and special time of intimate conversation and sharing with those He had chosen and those whom He truly and deeply loved. Greater detail and understanding of the bread (gifts and ministries) and wine (Holy Spirit flowing through us) can be found in our books *Holy How - Holiness, The Sabbath, Communion and Baptism* and in *God's Favorite Number*.

The Marriage Supper of the Lamb will be another time for intimate fellowship and love. It could be called "The First Supper," the beginning of a new era of intimate fellowship with His Bride. It will also be a celebration of the Passover Lamb, as we remember that without His Passover sacrifice, we would not be able to become His Bride for eternity.

GETHSEMANE

Before Jesus returns again to be crowned King of kings and Lord of lords, He won't be preparing for a cross and won't need to pray a "Gethsemane Prayer." What I see from this segment of His story is that Jesus had a hard time getting His most committed disciples to intercede for one hour. However, at His SECOND COMING, many millions of

A Powerful Prophetic Type and Shadow

intercessors will have been interceding and praying for His return.

THE MAIN EVENT - JESUS IS CROWNED KING

Let's start in **Luke 22:52-53:**

22:52 *"Then Jesus said to the chief priests, captains of the temple, and the elders who had come to Him, 'Have you come out, as against a robber, with swords and clubs?*
22:53 *When I was with you daily in the temple, you did not try to seize Me. But this is your hour, and the power of darkness.'"*

Please notice who arrested Jesus in verse 52. It was the religious leaders, functioning as civil or political leaders behind His arrest. They were the ones who were supposedly the "very holiest" among the people, but the most controlled by the evil one. They represent those in society today who pretend to care about the people, but they are more concerned with their own prosperity and power.

In Luke 23, they lead Jesus to Pilate, who represents the Kingdom of Rome. The Caesar in Rome was an earthly king of kings, but can be symbolic of God, who is the eternal King of kings in Heaven, as well as over all the earth. Notice in Daniel 7:13, which was quoted earlier, that they bring "One like the Son of Man to the Ancient of Days." Thus, bringing Jesus before Pilate, who represented an earthly king of kings, is a type or shadow of bringing Jesus before the Father for justice and judgment.

In Luke 23:4, *"Pilate said to the chief priests and the crowd, 'I find no fault in this Man.'"* The Father in Heaven would surely agree.

Pilate wanted no responsibility in this matter, and when he heard that Herod was in town, he sent Jesus to him. Herod was the Jewish king under Caesar, and he had jurisdiction over Galilee, where Jesus was from. Herod was delighted to see Jesus, having heard so much about him.

THE FIRST ROYAL ROBE

When Jesus refused to answer questions, Herod and his "men of war" treated Him with contempt and mocked Him. They "arrayed Him in a gorgeous robe" and sent Him back to Pilate (Luke 23:11).

THE SECOND ROYAL ROBE, A CROWN OF THORNS, AND BOWING THE KNEE

Pilate finally gave up trying to protect Jesus and gave Him over to the Jews and the soldiers. Many events related to the trial of Jesus and His crucifixion are detailed in **Matthew 27:27-31:**

A Powerful Prophetic Type and Shadow

27:27 "Then the soldiers of the governor took Jesus into the Praetorium and gathered the whole garrison around Him.
27:28 And they stripped Him and put a scarlet robe on Him.
27:29 When they had twisted a crown of thorns, they put it on His head, and a reed in His right hand. And they bowed the knee before Him and mocked Him, saying, 'Hail, King of the Jews!'
27:30 Then they spat on Him, and took the reed and struck Him on the head.
27:31 And when they had mocked Him, they took the robe off Him, put His own clothes on Him, and led Him away to be crucified."

Lots to unpack here, but briefly, this is what I see:

1. Jesus was given a scarlet robe – representing the blood He would shed, but also the glorious beauty of His coming Kingdom.
2. He received a painful crown of thorns – representing the great and glorious crown that He will receive after He returns to earth.
3. The soldiers bowed the knee, saying, "Hail, King of the Jews." This act was prophetic of what Paul declares in **Philippians 2:9-11:**

   2:9 Therefore God also has highly exalted Him and given Him the name which is above every name,

The Glorious Return of King Jesus

> 2:10 That at the name of Jesus, EVERY KNEE SHOULD BOW, of those in Heaven, and of those on earth, and of those under the earth,
> 2:11 And that every tongue should confess that Jesus Christ is Lord, to the glory of God the Father.

The first robe was given to Jesus by a Jewish King, indicating that the Jews will be the first to recognize Jesus as King. The second robe was given to Him by the Gentiles, to whom the gospel came after it was rejected by His own people. But I believe it will be the Jews who will be the most excited for their Messiah to return, because Jesus will be recognized as their Messiah before then.

THE CROSS AND THE SIGN

Jesus was finally led to Golgotha where He was crucified. The cross was His throne in this mock coronation, but it was the completion of the prophetic type and shadow of His SECOND COMING. As horrible and painful as it was to carry our sins, both physically and spiritually, how much more glorious will His coronation be when He returns to earth!

The sign that Pilate insisted on placing over Jesus' head proclaimed, "THIS IS THE KING OF THE JEWS." After His SECOND COMING, the sign that will be over Jesus' throne will say something like: "THIS IS THE KING OF KINGS AND LORD OF LORDS, AND HE SHALL REIGN FOREVER."

A Powerful Prophetic Type and Shadow

KING DAVID'S REIGN AS A TYPE AND SHADOW OF JESUS' MILLENIAL REIGN

In 1 Chronicles 12, we have a wonderful picture of the future reign of Jesus on the earth. David had already ruled for a few years over Judah (the Jews), while the rest of the tribes of Israel served the sons of King Saul after Saul's death. In 1 Chronicles 12, we have the record of each of the tribes of Israel coming to David and proclaiming him their king. In doing so, they pledged the support of their military forces.

Let me quote two of my favorite verses from this chapter:

1 Chronicles 12:18	*"Then the Spirit came upon Amasai, chief of the captains, and he said, 'We are yours, O David; We are on your side, O son of Jesse! Peace, peace to you, and peace to your helpers! For your God helps you.'*
1 Chronicles 12:38	*All these men of war, who could keep ranks, came to Hebron with a loyal heart, to make David king over all Israel; and all the rest of Israel were of one mind to make David king."*

I can picture the kings, presidents and prime ministers of every nation coming to submit themselves to King Jesus and to offer their entire military might for His use. What a glorious event that would be!!!

ONE MORE THING

This chapter has included a number of types and shadows, and I acknowledge that it is my opinion. And like many prophetic passages, these insights are something we need to ask confirmation on from the Holy Spirit.

While I'm on this track, let me suggest one more thing that seems to make sense to me. I believe that the Marriage Supper of the Lamb could be held on earth before an official Coronation Ceremony for Jesus. I believe there could be an official Wedding Ceremony first, followed by a Wedding Feast, where Jesus takes us as His legal bride. That would make us His Queen, with the legal authority to rule and reign with Him.

In summary, there were several days between Jesus' first entry into Jerusalem and His crucifixion. In the time period between His FIRST COMING and His burial, Jesus:

1. Cleansed the temple.
2. Healed the sick.
3. Taught the people.
4. Judged the Scribes and Pharisees.
5. Had the Last Supper.
6. Received Royal Robes from both Jews and Gentiles.
7. Received a Crown.
8. Received homage - the bowing of the knee to Him.

A Powerful Prophetic Type and Shadow

9. Was put on a rugged cross - His throne.
10. Had a sign over His head, stating He was King of the Jews.

At this point, I rest my case.

CHAPTER EIGHT

WHERE ARE WE NOW? COMFORTING CONCLUSIONS

I have no doubt that many who have read to this point could use a little more encouragement regarding the future as we have described it in this short book. I will do my best to encourage and build your faith and trust in the Great Shepherd, who promised never to leave us or forsake us. Let us always remember that whenever we go through tests and trials, He is always there with us, and we are always more than conquerors through Him who loves us.

GOD'S AGENDA

As one who has been in tune with major prophetic voices over the past number of decades, I can say with significant confidence that, without setting dates, a great harvest is the next major event on God's agenda. It has already begun, and it will reach a huge segment of society. The number stated by some of the most reputable prophets is one billion souls, mostly youth.

Where Are We Now? Comforting Conclusions

Just recently, we have seen an explosion of God's presence and glory on many university campuses, churches, and schools, just as many prophets have been prophesying. People from all over the world are coming to experience it. Awesome revivals are also happening in a number of other nations. Just in the past few days, I've heard about great moves of God in Uganda, Israel, and the Philippines, with thousands coming to Christ. Many churches are experiencing revival in America and the news media has been reporting some of the extraordinary events.

I believe that the antichrist spirit is definitely at work. Globalists are the tools in the enemy's hands to bring in this evil antichrist kingdom from hell. However, God is definitely restraining and sabotaging his plan with this awesome Great Awakening. In 2 Chronicles 20:22, we read that God ambushed the Coalition of Evil, or the enemies of Judah under Jehoshaphat, and they were defeated. God is now ambushing the current Coalition of Evil, composed of the globalist billionaires, the mainstream media, along with social media giants, the entertainment industry, and the political establishment.

God also has another prophetic promise to fulfill, and it will be right on time to fund His harvest. It's the long-awaited-for "transfer of wealth" from the wicked to the righteous. I say with complete confidence, that the transfer of wealth is on the way, and it will be in time to fund the gospel going into every part of the world. It will be far greater than you have imagined.

The antichrist will have to wait. God has His own plans and they come first. However, there will come a time after the harvest, when God separates the wheat from the chaff. This could be the Great Tribulation, a time where the faith of many young converts is tested and purified, as the Bride of Christ makes herself ready. But that probably won't be in my lifetime or yours. So, let's get on with Heaven's agenda and press in for a greater harvest than this world has ever seen.

WHY THE GREAT TRIBULATION WON'T BE SO TERRIBLE FOR JESUS' DISCIPLES

While there may be a season of physical suffering or deprivation for the followers of Jesus, there will never be a deprivation of His Presence. The Comforter, the Holy Spirit, will always be there, providing us with both His Fruit and Spiritual Gifts. When you think about it, having the gift of knowledge will be huge for those who know their God during that time. God will show His saints what the enemy's plans are so they can be thwarted, but they will also be able to see God do supernatural miracles among them.

When Daniel says the antichrist will have dominion over them, that doesn't mean over their minds or hearts. It means political control of their environment and access to facilities, resources, etc. He cannot stop the miracles and healings from occurring among the saints. They will continue to encourage one another prophetically and with words of wisdom. Some may die as martyrs, as in the

Where Are We Now? Comforting Conclusions

early church. Like those who have gone before them, their rewards are great in Heaven.

Here are a few important items to remember:

1. *"GOD IS OUR REFUGE AND STRENGTH, A VERY PRESENT HELP IN TIME OF TROUBLE"* (PSALM 46:1).
2. THERE ARE 365 "FEAR NOTS" IN SCRIPTURE – ONE FOR EACH DAY.
3. *"SAY TO THOSE WHO ARE FEARFUL-HEARTED, 'BE STRONG, DO NOT FEAR! BEHOLD, YOUR GOD WILL COME WITH VENGEANCE, WITH THE RECOMPENSE OF GOD, HE WILL COME AND SAVE YOU'"* (ISAIAH 35:4).
4. *"AND THUS WE SHALL ALWAYS BE WITH THE LORD. THEREFORE COMFORT ONE ANOTHER WITH THESE WORDS"* (1 THESSALONIANS 4:17-18).

When the antichrist does his evil thing for three and a half years, God's people will know that his time is ending. They can actually get excited, because they know that Jesus is on His way, and nothing can stop His plans from coming to fruition.

"The sufferings of this present time are not worthy to be compared with the glory which shall be revealed in us" (Romans 8:18).

The Glorious Return of King Jesus

LOST IN HIS GLORY

Finally, for those who still fear the suffering that could come with persecution for either yourself or future generations, I want to point out something that I firmly believe.

There is special grace for those who are called to special suffering. I say this not only from a biblical perspective, but from testimonies I've heard from people who underwent physical suffering and persecution. I believe that God will give special grace to His saints and surround them in a cloud of His glory, so they won't feel the pain that they would have otherwise. Let's just look at the stoning of Stephen in **Acts 7:55-60:**

7:55 *"But he, being full of the Holy Spirit, gazed into Heaven and saw the glory of God, and Jesus standing at the right hand of God,*

7:56 *And said, 'Look! I see the Heavens opened and the Son of Man standing at the right hand of God!'*

7:57 *Then they cried out with a loud voice, stopped their ears, and ran at him with one accord;*

7:58 *And they cast him out of the city and stoned him. And the witnesses laid down their clothes at the feet of a young man named Saul.*

7:59 *And they stoned Stephen as he was calling on God and saying, 'Lord Jesus, receive my spirit.'*

Where Are We Now? Comforting Conclusions

> 7:60   Then he knelt down and cried out with a loud voice, 'Lord, do not charge them with this sin.' And when he had said this, he fell asleep."

Before the stoning, God gave Stephen a Heavenly anesthetic by taking him into His glory in a vision. When the stoning did take place, rather than screaming in pain, Stephen was communicating with Jesus and asking God to not charge his persecutors with his death. Stoning would normally be an incredibly painful way to die, but Stephen was in another place where the pain was not as real as God's presence.

I remember hearing a testimony many years ago of a young man who was beaten for his faith. He said that he knew there was pain happening, but it was meaningless, because He felt the presence of God and the pain could not steal his joy. More recently, I've heard from special friends in Africa that when they were experiencing incredible persecution, their love for Jesus only deepened. They worshiped God with overwhelming joy because they were comforted by His presence.

And now, I pray off of every reader any fear and excessive focus on the antichrist. He's not really that big a deal; his time will be short. We will rule and reign with Jesus for one thousand years and then spend all of eternity with Him. Remember to read Daniel seven concerning the courtroom events.

The Glorious Return of King Jesus

RAPTURE DREAMS

Recently, I've noticed on social media a number of testimonies of people who have had what they have labeled "Rapture Dreams." I don't doubt the authenticity or integrity of those who have had these dreams. But after listening to some of their stories, I have found a common thread.

These dreams usually end with the dreamer and others rising up into the air to meet Jesus. They see His glory and experience various forms of emotional ecstasy. From what I have heard, they have not experienced going back to Heaven with Jesus. It's all about them rising out of their earthly bodies to meet Him in the air.

To be clear, we will never argue with the teaching that when Jesus comes, we will ascend from the earth and meet Jesus in the air. Our argument is with those who say we go back to Heaven with Him to escape the Great Tribulation. What happens back on the earth when we go up? We can't say with any scriptural authority; we can only imagine, as many have done in the rapture movies. Will there be chaos and disasters when Christians are driving cars or buses, or piloting planes? We might have to wait and see about that one.

What we do know is that when Jesus returns to earth, He will destroy the antichrist with *"the breath of His mouth and the brightness of His coming"* (2 Thessalonians 2:8). I can't say if the evil followers of the antichrist will experience the same fate at that time, but they will also be judged in God's timing.

LET'S REVIEW BRIEFLY OUR EIGHT DISCOVERIES

1. We found that the phrase "Left Behind" was not in the Bible in any end-time passage. In fact, the common use of the "Days of Noah" teaching by Jesus has had a backwards application. Those who were "left" are seen as those who missed out, when Jesus clearly meant they were spared, as Noah and family were spared death. Those who were taken are not those who are raptured, but those who are destroyed by God's judgment.

2. We dealt with the "Last Trumpet" dilemma. For there to be an Escape Rapture, there had to be another trumpet after the "Last Trumpet." We compared the three main "return of Jesus" passages and concluded that they all referred to the same event. Jesus will return only once, not twice.

3. Every end-time passage speaks about "His Coming," not "Our Going." If the New Testament writers had believed in an escape rapture, they would have spoken considerably more about it to comfort the saints. However, they only spoke about Jesus returning to the earth and being ready for that event.

4. We dealt with some unanswered questions in Daniel and Revelation regarding the antichrist and the

authority he was given to rule over the saints until the courts were seated, and then the saints of God were given the authority to rule. In Revelation 7, we find a great multitude, more than any man could number, who had been through great tribulation. They had suffered hunger, thirst, and heat from the sun, etc. The unanswered question is, why did this huge multitude of saints go through this tribulation, if Jesus had raptured all the saints just before it took place? To say they got saved during the tribulation, during persecution, is not easy to believe and has no scriptural backing to support it.

5. We disputed the theory that the "one who is taken out of the way" was the Holy Spirit. And we believe that the One who was restrained until the time was right was actually Jesus. We shared that the Greek grammar did not specify the antecedent to the pronoun "he" in more than one case, and it was up to the context to interpret who the "he" referred to. This author believes the Bible translators erred in the way they interpreted the context.

6. We also disputed a couple of other arguments made by the escape rapture theorists. The first was the "not appointed to wrath" argument. We showed that the "wrath" referred to in 1 Thessalonians 5:9 was actually speaking about God's judgment on sin, not the tribulation brought on by the antichrist. The second argument was the "open door" argument from Revelation 4:1. We saw this argument as a big

stretch and the result of not being able to find any credible reference to the rapture in the entire book of Revelation.

7. We showed how strong a prophetic type and shadow was portrayed by Jesus coming into Jerusalem as the Passover Lamb. He was accompanied by His disciples and a great multitude; another great multitude came out of the city to meet Him. They ushered Him into the city with a "Royal Procession." He was given Royal Robes, a Crown and a Throne with a sign that read "JESUS OF NAZARETH, THE KING OF THE JEWS." Many other details were prophetic of His second coming, including His judging of the religious and financial abusers of His people.

8. We finish up with our beliefs as to where we are in God's calendar and why we should not fear the end-time events. We will always have God's presence and power with us. He will still perform miracles and we will still hear His voice. We will have the fruit and the gifts of the Holy Spirit manifesting among us. There will be unprecedented unity and love flowing among the believers as things draw near the conclusion of this age.

And now, let's focus on how we can be ready for any end-time scenario.

A WORD TO THOSE WHO WANT TO KNOW JESUS AS LORD, SAVIOR, AND FRIEND:

If you have read this book, but don't have a personal relationship with Jesus, I encourage you to pray a prayer from your heart. He's been waiting for you and wants to meet you. He knows everything about you and yet He loves you passionately. His arms are wide open to you right now, just come as you are. Talk to Him as someone who is right there with you because He is. Tell Him you're sorry for all your sins and failures and for not accepting Him sooner. Thank Him for dying on the cross and for shedding His blood as a sacrifice for your sins. Tell Him, you accept His free gift with a grateful heart, and you want to love Him and serve Him the rest of your days. Tell Him that you want to be filled with His Holy Spirit to give you power over sin and temptation and the supernatural courage to tell others about His love. Thank Him for coming to live in your heart through the Holy Spirit. Then just worship and praise Him for saving you from your past sins and from a terrible future.

FINALLY, ONE MORE SCRIPTURE TO ENCOURAGE YOU: **PSALM 27:14:**

"WAIT ON THE LORD; BE OF GOOD COURAGE, AND HE SHALL STRENGTHEN YOUR HEART; WAIT I SAY ON THE LORD!"

AMEN!!!

Ben R. Peters

Ben R. Peters has been a student of the Word since he could read it for himself. He has a heritage of grandparents and parents who lived by faith and taught him the value of faith. That faith produced many miracle answers to prayer in their family life, as Ben and his wife, Brenda, have shared over 55 years of marriage and gospel ministry. Together they founded Kingdom Sending Center, in northern Illinois, and travel extensively, teaching and ministering prophetically to thousands each year. Their books are available on most e-readers, all other normal book outlets, as well as their website: www.kingdomsendingcenter.org.

Other Books Written by Ben R. Peters:
1. A Mandate to Laugh
2. Birthing the Book Within You
3. The Boaz Blessing
4. Catching Up to the Third World
5. Cinco Ministeriors En Un Poderoso Equipo
6. Faith on Fire
7. Finding Your Place on Your Kingdom Mountain
8. Folding Five Ministries into One Powerful Team
9. God is So God!
10. God's Favorite Number
11. Go Ahead, Be So Emotional
12. Holy How?
13. Holy Passion – Desire on Fire
14. Humility and How I Almost Achieved It
15. The Kingdom-Building Church
16. Kings & Kingdoms
17. The Marriage Anointing
18. Ministry Foundations 101
19. Prophetic Ministry -Strategic Key to the Harvest
20. Resurrection! A Manual for Raising the Dead
21. Signs and Wonders - To Seek or Not to Seek
22. The Ultimate Convergence
23. Veggie Village and the Great & Dangerous Jungle
24. With Me

Highlights of These Books Follow:

A Mandate to Laugh

Overcoming the Sennacherib Spirit

In this book you will learn about the demonic power that possessed Sennacherib and how it is influencing our society and political powers today. The clear and sinister purpose of the Sennacherib spirit is to control all people and nations for personal glory, power and profit. Yet, there is still hope God is not finished with the world!

Birthing the Book Within You

Inspiration and Practical Help to Produce Your Own Book

Writing and publishing your own book has never been easier, thanks to computer and digital printing technology. Ben R. Peters has been down this road many times, and now in this book, he shows how you can do it too. With spiritual insight and inspiration, he offers many practical tips to help you give birth to the book within you.

The Boaz Blessing

Releasing the Power of This Ancient Blessing Into Your World Today

The Boaz Blessing will give you courage as you dare to believe for the favor of God for yourself, for the people you love, and for the people who need to understand the mercy of their heavenly Father.

Catching Up to the Third World

Seven Indispensable Keys to Explosive Revival in the Western Church

Catching Up to the Third World reveals how God is provoking the Western Church to godly jealousy, to produce a powerful revival in the "First World" nations, so that the resources of the West can be most effectively utilized in the coming global harvest.

Cinco Ministerios En Un Poderoso Equipo

Llevando la Reforma Profetica y Apostolica Al Siguiente Nivel

Este libro da a la iglesia una visión de lo que podemos lograr cuando capacitamos a cada ministerio para hacer lo que mejor puede hacer como parte del equipo ministerial que Dios ha dado a la iglesia.

Faith on Fire

Dismantling Structures of Unbelief, Building Unshakeable Strongholds of Faith

Most Christians wonder why they don't see greater results from their prayers. In *Faith on Fire*, Ben R. Peters addresses these questions and identifies the structures of unbelief that may be keeping you in fear, doubt, and insecurity.

Finding Your Place on Your Kingdom Mountain

A Practical Guide and Workbook for Reigning as Kings in the Kingdom of God

In *Finding Your Place on Your Kingdom Mountain*, Ben R. Peters gives you practical help to discover on which of the "Seven Mountains" of society God wants you to display the rule and reign of His kingdom.

Folding Five Ministries into One Powerful Team

Taking the Apostolic and Prophetic Reformation to the Next Powerful Level

This book gives the Church a vision for what can be accomplished when we empower each ministry to do what it does best as part of the ministry team that God has given to the Church.

God is So God!

The Adventures of a Traveling Ministry on a Prophetic Faith Journey

Brenda Peters knows what it's like to launch out on a faith journey with only an RV for her home. This book, filled with her road adventures in a full-time traveling ministry, reveals the awesome power of God to intervene in every aspect of life. This is a unique book, full of faith stories and prophetic adventures that will touch your heart.

God's Favorite Number

The Secret Keys and
Awesome Power of True Unity

Does God have a favorite number? Yes, He does - so much so that you'll find it 1,969 times in Scripture. It's a number that relates to unity.

Go Ahead, Be So Emotional

***Empowering the Emotional Personality
To do Awesome Exploits for God***

It's time for all of God's emotionally expressive people to rise up and fulfill their destiny. In this book you will learn how to let the anointing of God come upon you as you use your emotional personality to take more territory for His kingdom.

Holy How?

Holiness, the Sabbath, Communion and Baptism

Enjoy the Privilege of Being Holy to the Lord! Believer, you are chosen to be special and unique and filled with the very nature of God, through your intimate relationship with the Father, Son, and Holy Spirit.

Holy Passion – Desire on Fire

Igniting The Torch of Godly Passion

God is a God of passion, and He is looking for a people with passion!

Humility and How I Almost Achieved It

UNCOVER A HIGHLY UNDERVALUED KEY TO LASTING SUCCESS AND KINGDOM POWER! You will learn the greatest shortcut to true humility, plus some practical ways to stay humble about being humble.

The Kingdom-Building Church

Experiencing the Explosive Potential of the Church in Kingdom-Building Mode

Come with Ben R. Peters and explore what the heart of God cries out for, what the plans of God are for His church, and what He can do when we allow Him to put us in Kingdom-building mode.

Kings and Kingdoms

**Anointing A New Generation of
Kings to Serve the King of Kings**

In *Kings and Kingdoms*, Ben R. Peters explores what it means to be a king under the authority of Jesus Christ and how you can truly "seek first the Kingdom of God" by fulfilling your role as king over the domain God has given you.

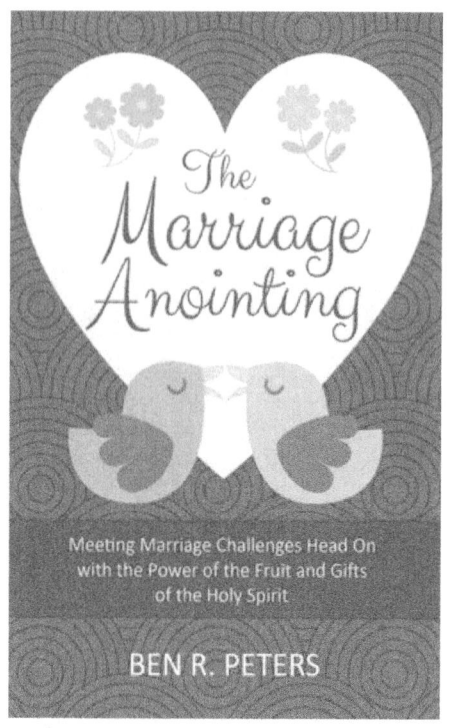

The Marriage Anointing

Meeting Marriage Challenges Head on with the Power of the Fruit and Gifts of the Holy Spirit

Meet your marriage challenges head on! There is no power from hell that can defeat two people who have learned to listen to God's voice and invite Him to bless them with everything He wants to bestow upon them. This book shows you how, with the "double-barreled" approach of the Fruit and Gifts of the Holy Spirit, your marriage can become a huge source of fulfillment for both partners and together become an awesome ministry team.

Ministry Foundations 101

Preparing the Saints for the Work of the Ministry

The goal of this study is to help you be the best possible stewards of the gifts, talents, knowledge, and experience that God has given to each of you.

Prophetic Ministry

Strategic Key to the Harvest

Ben R. Peters knows from first-hand experience the value and effectiveness of prophetic ministry as an evangelistic tool. Along with his wife Brenda, he has been doing prophetic ministry since 1999. He has seen countless salvations, healings, and miracles as a result.

Resurrection

A Manual for Raising the Dead

Let's Raise the Dead! Raising the dead is not for super-Christians but is in the DNA of every believer.

Signs and Wonders
To Seek or Not to Seek

Exploring The Power of the
Miraculous to Bring People to Christ

To Seek or Not to Seek? Signs and Wonders gives a clear and resounding answer to that controversial question. The conclusions of this thorough and fascinating investigation of the faith-making power of the miraculous will be difficult to refute.

The Ultimate Convergence

An End Times Prophecy of the Greatest Shock and Awe Display Ever to Hit Planet Earth

Convergence has been a hot buzzword in Kingdom streams for the past few years. Ben R. Peters believes that God is preparing for the greatest convergence of natural and spiritual elements of all time in preparation for His great harvest and the coming back to earth of His Beloved Son, Jesus Christ.

Veggie Village and the Great & Dangerous Jungle: An Allegory

When church becomes more of a religion than a relationship, it can seem like just eating our vegetables. We are told to do good things like read our Bibles, pray, and go to church because they are good for us - and they are. However, God wants to win the lost, and it is often not easy to get others to come and eat with us if we offer only vegetables.

With Me

With Me takes you on an incredible journey of discovery about the Lord Jesus, as it uncovers a refreshing new revelation from the most famous Psalm in Scripture.

All Books are Available from Kingdom Sending Center
www.kingdomsendingcenter.org

Printed in Great Britain
by Amazon